THE PURE WORDS OF GOD

Where to Find God's Words Which We Are Commanded to Receive and Keep

H. D. Williams, M.D., Ph.D.

THE OLD PATHS PUBLICATIONS
142 GOLD FLUME WAY
CLEVELAND, GEORGIA 30528

BIBLE FOR TODAY #3344

Disclaimer

The author of this work has quoted the writers of many articles and books. This does not mean that the author endorses or recommends the works of others. If the author quotes someone, it does not mean that he agrees with all of the author's tenets, statements, concepts, or words, whether in the work quoted or any other work of the author. There has been no attempt to alter the meaning of the quotes; and therefore, some of the quotes are long in order to give the entire sense of the passage.

Library of Congress Control Number: 2007942450
REL067030: Religion: Christian Theology – Apologetics.

ISBN 978-0-9801689-1-4

All Scripture quotes are from the King James Bible except those verses compared and then the source is identified.

Address All Inquiries To:
THE OLD PATHS PUBLICATIONS, Inc.
142 Gold Flume Way
Cleveland, Georgia, U.S.A. 30528

Web: www.theoldpathspublications.com
E-mail: TOP@theoldpathspublications.com

BIBLE FOR TODAY #3344
Web: www.biblefortoday.org
E-mail: bft@biblefortoday.org

1.0

DEDICATION

This work is dedicated to my five grandchildren who are a delight to their grandfather. It is his prayer that they will come to a full, unfeigned understanding and appreciation for the "pure" Words of our Great God and Saviour.

CONTENTS

ABBREVIATIONS

A = Codex Alexandrinus
A.D. = Anno Dei
AFT(s) = accurate and faithful translation(s)
Apographs = copies of the original manuscripts
ASV = American Standard Version
Autographs = original manuscripts
B = Codex Vaticanus
B.C. = Before Christ
ca. = circa
cf = compare
DE = dynamic equivalent or equivalence
DET(s)= dynamic equivalent translation(s)
e.g. = Latin, exempli gratia = for example
EL = essentially literal
Encarta = Encarta Online Dictionary
etc. = Latin, et cetera = and so forth
ESV = English Standard Version
FE = formal equivalent
FunE = functional equivalent
GTO = Greek Text of Origen
i.e. = Latin, id est = that is
ibid = Latin, ibidem = in the same place
Inerrant = containing no mistakes
ISBE = International Standard Bible Encyclopedia
KJB = King James Bible
LB = Living Bible
Lectionaries = a book containing portions of Scripture
Letter = Letter of Aristeas
LXX = Septuagint
MSS = manuscripts
MT = Hebrew Masoretic Text
NASB = New American Standard Version
NCV = New Century Version
NIV = New International Version
NLT = New Living Translation
NT = New Testament
op.cit. = Latin opera citato = in the work previously cited
OT = Old Testament
p., pp = page(s)
Plenary = full, complete, entire
Revision = re-examination for correction; as the revision of a

book or writing or of a proof sheet; a revision of statutes.
RSV = Revised Standard Version
RT = Received Texts
TEV = Todays English Version
TR = Textus Receptus
TT = Traditional Text
TT/RT = traditional text/received text
VE = verbal equivalent
VPI = verbal plenary inspiration (inspiration of all the words of God)
VPP = verbal plenary preservation (preservation of all the Words of God)
VPT = verbal plenary translating (translation of all the Words of God)
vid. supra = Latin, vide supra = See above or other material in this work
viz. = Latin, videlicet = namely
WH = Westcott and Hort, 1881

PREFACE

*"Now to him that is of power to stablish you according to my gospel, and the preaching of Jesus Christ, according to the revelation of the mystery, which was kept secret since the world began, But now is made manifest, and by the scriptures of the prophets, according to the commandment of the everlasting God, **made known to all nations** for the obedience of faith" (Romans 16:25-26).*

Do Not Change The King James Bible

Many people will immediately conclude from the work to follow on the "pure" Words of God that the author desires to change the King James Bible. There could be nothing further from the truth. Change without the need for change brings confusion. There has been enough confusion generated among believers in the churches of the world. The confusion has precipitated differing doctrines, dozens of denominations, the call for abandonment of the doctrine of separation from apostasy, the loss of a moral compass, and many other problems. The unnecessary "changes" manifested in the 'new bible' versions is enough to distress and confuse any saint who loves the Lord and His Words. What is the source of all of this turmoil? Could the inaccurate use of terms and labels such as pure and inspired by professors, pastors, and teachers be a leading cause for the frenzied running to and fro among seekers of God's Words in these last days?

Furthermore, the "derivative" 'new' translations precipitated by the modern and postmodern textual critics are notoriously appalling and have insidiously infected the majority of churches that claim to be His assembly. These churches will not recover from the damage before our Lord Jesus Christ returns.

The churches are too far along the road of apostasy to return to a Biblical standard. For example, consider the changes in the administration and organization of alleged churches, now called "communities," in the postmodern age.[1] Doctrine derived from God's truly pure, inspired, preserved Words is not expounded. The alleged "communities" of God's people are no longer compliant with the Words of God concerning MANY issues.

God's principles, laws, precepts, and doctrines are fixed; woe unto them who would change things important to God's predetermined and unchanging Contract with man. Changing God's pure, perfect, precise Words that determine doctrines, precepts, judgments, laws, testimonies, commandments, and government of His church is a deep abyss. Many are falling into it. God's warnings in Scripture are very clear concerning this pit (cf. Deut. 4:2, Pro. 30:5-6, Jer. 23:28, Rev. 22:18-19 and many other places). Technologies, cultures, government, and many other things may change, but not God's eternal ways. Many will claim that this author and others who hold these beliefs are old fashioned and rigid. The questions we ask are these, "Are your ways working?" "Are your church members growing in the knowledge and wisdom of God?" "If not, why not?" Perhaps God is not blessing your assemblies. Perhaps the Ancient of Days, who knows the heart of man, settled His God-breathed pure Words in eternity past for a reason. Do you know where they are?

The King James Bible Will Never Be Matched

The English King James Bible (KJB) will never be matched because of its literary genius and its accuracy and faithfulness to the

---

[1] H. D. Williams, *Hearing the Voice of God, Related to Revelation, Conscience, Inspiration, Illumination, and Postmodernism* (The Old Paths Publications, Cleveland, GA, 2008) Chapter 6—Postmodernism.

underlying proper Hebrew, Aramaic, and Greek Words. So why change? In addition, there are many practical reasons that changes should not and cannot be made in the greatest translation ever produced for the English-speaking world. They have to do with such things as:

1. costs,
2. inferior modern-day scholarship,
3. copyright, which demands that a certain number of words be changed in a book to obtain one, and
4. many other similar realistic problems.

Furthermore, the few archaic words in the King James Bible do not require change.[2] They can easily be learned. Subsequently, the man in the pew can read the same magnificent translation of the Words of God as everyone else in the English-speaking world. The local assembly can read the same words as the pastor in the pulpit. What could happen if pastors and teachers would use the best providentially created tool, the KJB, to assist them in their duty to bring unity in God's assemblies? There is nothing more confusing in a congregation than the use of different translations and paraphrases of corrupted original-language texts.

Furthermore, the language in the King James Bible is not the language that was spoken by the English-speaking people in the 15th or 16th centuries. Rather, it is a unique Bible language that accurately and faithfully reflects the pure, preserved, inspired, infallible, and inerrant Words of God. It is Bible-language.

It is documented that the language of the King James Bible is easier to read than the modern translations of corrupted texts. It is documented that children who use the King James Bible as the basis for their school curriculum score higher in achievement tests than other

---

[2] The Defined King James Bible, available from BibleForToday.org, defines the archaic words excellently.

students. It is documented that the King James Bible is the only Bible in the last 400 years that has precipitated a true revival in a nation or society. Why would any discerning student of the Words of God want to change the King James Bible?

Adam Clarke (1810) said:

> "Those who have compared most of the European translations with the original, have not scrupled to say, that the English translation of the Bible made under the direction of King James I, is the most accurate and faithful of the whole. Nor is this its only praise; THE TRANSLATORS HAVE SEIZED THE VERY SPIRIT AND SOUL OF THE ORIGINAL AND EXPRESSED THIS ALMOST EVERYWHERE WITH PATHOS AND ENERGY. The original, from which it was taken, is **alone superior** to the Bible which was translated by the authority of King James…Besides, our translators have not only made a standard translation, but they have made their translation the standard of our language…This is an opinion in which my heart, my judgment, and my conscience coincide (Adam Clarke, General Introduction to his Commentary on the Whole Bible, 1810-26)."[3] (my bolding and underlining, HDW).

The King James Bible is a beautiful flower that reflects the rich nourishment drawn from its roots. The roots of this flower are anchored in the Words of the Rock who provided the immutable Words of Truth (Deut. 32:4, Eph. 2:20). The only thing that remains is for the sincere repentant soul, who is starved for the Words of eternal life, to trust and receive the inheritance; the fruit of the *"rose of Sharon"* and *"the lily of the valleys"* (Song 2:1)

---

[3] David Cloud, "The Peerless Literary Beauty of the King James Bible" from: *Faith vs. the Modern Bible Versions,* Way of Life Literature, Port Huron, MI, 2005, as quoted in Fundamental Baptist Information Service, 11/05/2007) p. 2

Innate, Inherent, Versus Inherited, Acquired

In the discussions to follow, the terms and concepts related to innate and inherent compared to inherit and acquire are important. God is an eternal being. He does not inherit or acquire abilities. He is not the product of a birth; he is not a creation. Therefore, God's power, authority, and characteristics are inherent or innate without any relationship to being born, created, or genetically made. His traits are inherent and not secondary to inherited abilities. His power and authority are not acquired or inherited; they are inherent. His abilities and character traits are not developed, learned, or conditioned by the environment. Therefore, we speak of God's power, authority, and knowledge as stemming from His omnipotence, omniscience, and omnipresence. We do not consider His knowledge, power, and authority as *derived* from any source. Nothing about God is a result of a *derivative*.

God's ability to cause or create miracles is inherent. A miracle is an event that occurs outside of or beyond the limits or laws of nature. Man cannot perform a miracle. He must operate within the laws of nature. God is not restrained or limited by the laws of nature. He created them. Providential events are akin to miracles, but are within the limits of physical laws. God can and does use providence to control His universe.

Similarly, God's ability to breath-out inspired Words is inherent. His innate or inherent ability, authority, and power to speak Words given by inspiration is not transferable to man, just as His ability to create or cause a miracle is not transferable to man. Man must operate within the laws of nature. God is beyond the restraint of nature in every way.

God can and does grant *"acquired authority or power"* to certain men (Apostles and prophets) to perform miracles, but the inherent ability is not transferrable. The inherent ability remains with God who alone has none of the restraints of man's dimensions. The Holy Spirit, who indwelt the Apostles, actually performed the miracles based on the *acquired authority (power)* granted to those 'certain' men (Acts 3:12).

In like fashion, God grants man the authority to translate His Words into the languages of the world. However, the innate power of inspiration inherent in God is not transferrable to man. Men simply recorded the original inspired Words breathed-out by the innate power of God. The men who recorded the Words were not inspired and did not possess the inherent power of God to inspire Words.

The inspired words given by an omniscient, omnipotent, and omnipresent God and translated into words chosen by man have *"acquired authority"* or *"acquired power."* The Words do not have the *innate or inherent power or authority* of the original inspired Words given by God. The 'original' Words of God are fixed, permanent, unchanging, inspired, inerrant, infallible, and preserved by His innate or inherent power. Therefore, we do not call the words chosen to translate the original Words of God inspired, although God grants acquired authority to them, if they are accurate and faithful translations of His Words. Surely, many people are aware of the diminished power present in dynamic equivalent translations when compared to the dynamic power of formal, verbal equivalent translations.

There Is No Derivative Inspiration Or Purity

Before considering the meaning of the "pure" Words of God, the next concept that must be addressed is derivative inspiration and derivative purity. Some people are attributing derivative inspiration and purity to translations. Many people teach that the King James Bible is derivatively inspired or pure. A derivative implies *change*. Synonyms of "derivative" are unoriginal, imitative, plagiaristic, copied, derived, lacking in originality, offshoot, by-product, spin-off, and end-product of something that is changing. The *antonym* of derivative is original. A derivative word in linguistics is a word formed from another word. The word is similar but can and usually does have a significantly different meaning. It is very likely not to be synonymous (e.g. adding a suffix or prefix to a word may change the meaning significantly). In calculus, a derivative is a measurement of how a value **changes** as its inputs **change**.

Since the Words of God are unchanging in their original pure, perfect, inspired "*jots and tittles*," **no** derivative can be formed. They are the original. Their 'value' or input is not changing from moment to moment or culture to culture. They are fixed. Translating is simply choosing a word among many possibilities in a receptor-language according to syntax that comes closest to the original-language word. It is not a derivative word, which implies change based on changing 'values,' but it is an accurate representation of the **fixed** inspired word. The best Biblical translation is a verbal and formal translation. This kind of translation matches as closely as possible the original, unchanging input. The input is the **fixed** "*foundation,*" the Words of God. This foundation is more reliable and fixed than the foundation of the largest skyscraper in the world. God's Words are fixed by an eternal, immutable, invisible, God and His immutable promises (1 Tim. 1:17, Heb. 6:18, 8:6, 13:8, 1 Pe. 1:4, 2 Pe. 3:9, 1 Jn. 2:25).

A derivative translation would be akin to a dynamic equivalent translation(s) which changes over time to suit evolving cultures. It would be more appropriate to call translations such as the NIV, NLT, and others, derivative translating. This is suggestive of a changing foundation. Imagine a changing skyscraper foundation. Eventually, the entire building would fall as a result. Is this why the dynamic equivalent translations adopted by churches around the world demonstrate "falling" doctrine?

A derivative is a function that **changes** from moment to moment because it is dependent upon variables. There is no variableness, or waxing, or waning with God or His Words (Heb. 13:8, Jam. 1:17). God and His Words are unchangeable. If we claim any translation has derivative inspiration and purity, we are essentially giving those who produce translations every six months in English and frequently in other languages the tacit approval to continue to produce changing 'derivatives' every six months. They may also assume the right to claim their 'new' derivative translation is inspired and pure, which many are presently doing, as we shall see. Where will it stop? Besides, it is a misnomer to claim derivative inspiration for a translation, because the input, which is the Words from God, is fixed. These misunderstandings of inspiration, derivative inspiration, inherent, inherited, innate, and acquired are causing monstrous problems.

For example, the following quotes are from men who are incorrectly claiming derivative inspiration of translations. Dr. Thomas Cassidy said:

> "The year before I had presented a paper that dealt with the doctrine of derivative inspiration. I believe translations are inspired in the derivative sense. That is, the history of the translation is inspired history, the promises are inspired promises, and the prophecy is inspired prophecy. In the plenary sense a bible translation can be said to be inspired, but not in the verbal sense. That has been the orthodox position for several centuries, possibly for a couple of millennia."[4]

---

[4] Dr. D. A. Waite, Th.D., Ph.D., "Dr. Waite's Reply to Dr. Cassidy" (http://www.deanburgonsociety.org/DBS_Society/waite_reply.htm) accessed 11/01/07.

Where Dr. Cassidy goes astray is assigning inspiration to history, promises, and prophecy. This is very similar to the claim that God left us a message and not specific, precise Words. God breathed the **Words.** They are the original Hebrew, Aramaic, and Greek inspired Words. They were given once (Jude 1:3). He did not inspire history, providence, promises, or prophecy. Furthermore, this author cannot find any proof that derivative inspiration is an **orthodox** position for several centuries or from ancient times. Another website maintained by "Baptistpillars" has another article by Dr. Cassidy, which discusses derivative inspiration. Again, no documentation of "historical" orthodox support for a "derived" idea could be found.

Dr. Ken Matto and others make similar statements about inspiration. They are good brothers, but perhaps they have not thought through their claims or they are attempting to be mediators and 'to sooth ruffled feathers.' We agree that accurate and faithful translations carry imputed or acquired authority, but they are not inspired by imputation. Inspiration is a very special process and product of God, which cannot be transferred and cannot be applied to man's productions. Dr. Matto said:

> "Since the King James Bible is based on these pure manuscripts, this authority is imputed to the KJV and is evident because people are still getting saved and lives are changed through the teaching and preaching of the King James Bible…God's Word is preserved for us in the King James Bible and although not inspired as the original autographs were, they carry the authority of the original autographs. **We can also refer to it as "imputed or derivative inspiration"** since the King James Bible carries as much authority as the original manuscripts did. Let me repeat, the difference between preservation and inspiration is, inspiration was when God penned the original manuscripts through the holy men of old and preservation is the keeping of those manuscripts down through time. I hope this clears up the misconception of an "Inspired Translation." The King James Bible is a guided translation of the

manuscripts handed down to us which had its birth in the
original manuscripts which God gave with appended Divine
authority."[5]

Conferred Authority or Inspiration?

There is **no** comparison of **imputed** authority to alleged
derivative or imputed inspiration. God cannot impute the ability to
inspire Words anymore than He can impute the innate or inherent ability
to perform miracles. Similarly, imputed righteousness resulting from faith
in the completed work of Christ on the Cross of Calvary is not innate in
man. It is conferred righteousness. Similarly, authority is conferred upon
a representative by a superior authority, but not inherent inspiration or
the innate ability to perform miracles. Again, inspiration refers solely to
the original and preserved God-breathed Words, which were recorded by
the prophets and Apostles.

An Example

For example, a policeman has authority conferred upon him by
the laws of a society to hold up his hand and stop a speeding semi-tractor
and trailer, but he does not have sufficient power or strength to stop the
vehicle. Similarly, authority is conferred upon an accurate, faithful,
verbal, formal translation, but not inspiration. Furthermore, the power,
muscle, strength, or ability to perform miracles rested with God; it could
not be transferred to the prophets or Apostles, but they were granted
conferred power or authority **at times**. Without reliance on conferred
authority, the policeman mentioned above or the Apostles and prophets
would have no power. In other words, power can be (1) authority

---

[5] Dr. Ken Matto, "Is the King James Bible Inspired?"
(http://www.scionofzion.com/kjvinsp.htm) accessed 11/01/07.

conferred upon others or (2) inherent power such as that authority and power possessed by God. Similarly, inspiration was not conferred upon the Apostles and prophets. The recorders of the inspired Words of God were not inspired themselves. They were simply the agents God chose to record the Words. The men were **not** inspired. In other words, they could not speak inspired Words nor have the inherent power to speak inspired Words. Only God has that kind of power and ability. Paul said:

> *"Which things also we speak, not in the **words** which man's wisdom teacheth, but which the Holy Ghost teacheth; comparing spiritual things with spiritual"* (1 Corinthians 2:13).

The King James Bible is Not Inspired

Every person holding the view that the King James Bible is inspired, derivatively inspired, derivatively pure, or derivatively perfect is not only linguistically and historically incorrect, he is theologically incorrect. Furthermore, the authority of the King James Bible is conferred upon it by the inherent power of a Holy God, who commanded translations (Rom. 16:25-27, 1 Cor. 14:21). Therefore, the King James Bible has acquired power, because of the inherent power behind it. Its power is evident from changed lives. This is similar to the authority of the Apostles to perform miracles. Lives were changed; bodies were healed; people were brought back to life; other similar events occurred, all because God conferred authority and power; not because of inherent or innate power and authority. The Apostles and prophets were representatives of God, similar to a "representative" policeman. The King James Bible is a "representative" of God's inspired Words.

Calling a Translation Inspired Causes Confusion

A person calling any translation inspired is simply adding to the widespread and growing confusion facing churches in these last days. Certainly, many people have been seeking new ideas or other ways to exalt the glory of the Words of God and the **conferred** authority of accurate and faithful translations, but there has been a muddying of the "pure water" and confusion as to where the "pure" Words are found.

It is hoped that men would drop their use of the words inspired and pure to refer to any translation because of the tremendous confusion that is generated by these claims. The claims cannot be supported by a careful examination of the Biblical meaning of the words inspiration and pure in the Bible. Furthermore, great scorn is generated around the world by the false claims of inspiration and purity for the English Bible only. Lastly, the incorrect application of these terms is transferring God's innate power and character to man. In effect, it is transferring God's glory to man by claiming man's translations are equivalent to the God-breathed Words.

Proper Use of Inspiration, Pure, and Authority Will Generate Student Interest in the Original-Language Words of the Bible

Hopefully, proper definitions and application of the words will once again motivate more students to study the original languages of Hebrew, Aramaic, and Greek. This desire has been lost over the last several centuries. Now, a plumber, electrician, fireman, construction worker, doctor, lawyer, etc., who has no training at all in the original languages and who desires to "preach," takes his place in the pulpit and begins to proclaim his improper exegesis that is based upon his thoughts and emotions. They have far too often gone awry. This does not mean a pastor/teacher has to be an expert linguist, but he should at least have the tools to use Hebrew and Greek lexicons and dictionaries. We remember Paul's commandment to Timothy, his son in the faith:

> *"Thou therefore, my son, be strong in the grace that is in Christ Jesus. And the things that thou hast heard of me among many witnesses, the same commit thou to **faithful** men, **who shall be able to teach others** also"* (2 Timothy 2:1-2).

Paul said, *"that thou hast heard of me."* He spoke Koiné Greek, which was the common-language of the Roman Empire while Latin was the trade-language. These verses (2 Tim. 2:1-2) are a strong statement that relates to the proper training of men who would desire to be teachers because *"they...must give account"*:

> *"...they watch for your souls, as **they that must give account**, that they may do it with joy, and not with grief: for that is unprofitable for you"* (Hebrews 13:17).

H. D. Williams, M.D., Ph.D.

CHAPTER 1

THE PURE WORDS OF GOD

*"The words of the LORD are **pure** words: **as** silver tried in a furnace of earth, purified seven times"*(Psalms 12:6).

*"Every word of God is **pure**: he is a shield unto them that put their trust in him"* (Proverbs 30:5).

Introduction

Many students of the Words of God have noticed a connection between the doctrines of *"inspiration"* and *"preservation."* If God inspired His Words, He would not abandon them; He would watch over them and preserve them for each generation as He promised. What has not been noticed by many students is a similar principle: If God inspired and preserved His Words, He would not allow any of His Words to be destroyed, corrupted, tainted, added to, changed, subtracted from, or the order of the Words to be altered. He would ***keep*** them *"**pure**"* because they are His Words and they are the *"foundation"* for making His doctrines known to other nations through translations of them.

In other words, the doctrine of inspiration is vitally linked to the doctrines of preservation **and** purity of the original language Words of God. Those Words were God-breathed in the Hebrew, Aramaic, and Greek and available and preserved for their accurate and faithful translations into the languages of the world. God did not leave us an inaccurate or imprecise message, concept, or thought. Dr. Jack Moorman highlights these issues in one of his recent works:

"The Authorized Version of the Scripture is the
receptus of doctrinal truth. It is fuller and more distinct

doctrinally than any other version. The first profitable outcome of inspiration is doctrine (II Tim. 3:16). The first purpose of Scripture is to establish doctrine. It is not surprising that the doctrinal heart of Scripture should have borne the fury of Satan's attack through the centuries, and especially during the Second and Third. A number of early witnesses show the scars of this warfare in disfiguring, defacing and deletion of doctrinal truth. God, however, has been faithful to His promise and there has always been a **Traditional Text** in which ***truth remained pure and full***."[6] [my bolding, HDW).

The Traditional Text refers to the original God-breathed Hebrew, Aramaic, and Greek preserved Words. The Words are pure and perfect.

In regard to the Scriptures, there are many questions that have arisen over the last several centuries concerning the use of the word "*pure*." It appears anything and everything may be called pure. For example, a recent popular book by Susan Johnson is called "*Pure Sin*." Others attribute pure to the imagination, to drivel, to mathematics, to a lily, to desire, to sex, to lust, to sunsets, to style, to temptation, or to taste.[7]

What is "pure" Scripture? How is "*pure*" defined in this situation? How is it defined when referring to other entities? For example, what is "*pure gold*"?[8] A metallurgist considers 10 parts contamination in a thousand parts, which is 24 carat gold, as pure gold. By calling something "*pure*," can we mean a little less than perfect with a little contamination?

---

[6] J. A. Moorman, *Early Manuscripts, Church Fathers, and the Authorized Versions with Manuscript Digests and Summaries* (Bible For Today Press, Collingswood, NJ, 2005) 9.
[7] There are numerous books at Albris.com that are given these titles. Simply type in their search engine the word "pure."
[8] Gold is expressed in carats (ct) of purity from 9 to 24 or as parts per thousand 375 = (9 ct) to 990 = (24 ct). Pure gold is usually designated 24 ct or 990 parts per thousand, but please note that it still contains at least 10 parts of contaminant. (Reference: AZOM.com; http://www.azom.com/Details.asp?ArticleID=2430) accessed 10/14/07.

Does pure mean complete as used in pure filth? If something is pure is it perfect and precise? Is something pure that is accurate and faithful? Accuracy has many definitions; an accurate measurement may have many acceptable tolerances depending on the application.

For instance, will the *"city of God"* that comes down from heaven have a little bit of contamination in its gold? The *"great city, the holy Jerusalem, descending out of heaven from God"* and the *"street of the city"* will be *"pure gold"* (Rev. 21:10, 18, 21, Heb. 11:10). Is the *"pure gold"* of the street and city 990 parts in 1000 (24 carats), or is it 1000 parts in 1000 gold?

Applying this same question to Scripture, C. H. Spurgeon said:

> "But this is the Word of God; come, search, ye critics, and find a flaw; examine it, from its Genesis to its Revelation, and find an error. This is a vein of pure gold, **unalloyed** by quartz, or any earthly substance."[9] (my emphasis, HDW)

Which words was Spurgeon referring to as pure?

Likewise, Scripture speaks of a "pure heart:"

> *"Blessed are the **pure in heart**: for they shall see God"* (Matthew 5:8). *"Seeing ye have purified your souls in obeying the truth through the Spirit unto unfeigned love of the brethren, see that ye love one another with a **pure heart** fervently"* (1 Peter 1:22).

Does this mean completely uncontaminated like the heart of our Lord Jesus Christ? Such a heart in man is not possible, according to Scripture:

> *"The heart is deceitful above all things, and desperately wicked: who can know it?"* (Jeremiah 17:9, cf. Rom. 3:23, Isa. 53:6).

---

[9] C. H. Spurgeon, "The Immutability of God—Sermon 1" (*The Spurgeon Sermon Collection*, The Masters Christian Library, Ages Software, 2000) 104.

We Are Required to Show the Difference
Between Pure and Purified

The examples given in the Old Testament are for our learning in this age (1 Cor. 10:6). Therefore, man must be exceptionally careful that he does not carry out or participate in six very significant warnings from our God given in the Old Testament. Jehovah repeatedly warns:

1. Do not violate my law (Words),
2. Do not profane or blaspheme my holy sanctuary[10] or holy things,
3. Do not fail to be aware that there is a **difference** between pure and impure things; between the clean and the unclean; between common things and holy things,
4. Do not fail **to show others** that there is a **difference** between pure or holy things and impure or unholy things,
5. Do not pretend to hide your eyes from my commandments,
6. Do not take my name in vain and disrespect or blaspheme, wound, pollute, stain, or defile it or my Words.

The warnings are throughout the Old Testament, but they are summarized in one verse in Ezekiel. The Lord said:

---

[10] A saint (believer) in this age is the sanctuary for our God (Jn. 14:17, 23, Rom. 8:9, 11, 12:1-3, 1 Cor. 3:16 = temple, house, dwelling place, or sanctuary; etc.)

> *"Her priests have violated my law, and have profaned mine holy things: they have put no* **_difference_** *between the* **holy** *and profane, neither have they* **_shewed difference_** *between the unclean and the* **clean**, *and have hid their eyes from my sabbaths, and I am profaned among them"* (Ezekiel 22:26).

The word, "*clean*," in this verse is the Hebrew word, חהור (tahowr), which is translated pure in many verses (e.g. Pro. 15:26). It seems that only "clean" or "pure" animals, that is, those animals **without** defects and in **no** need of "cleaning,' could be used in sacrifices in the tabernacle or temple of God as there is a difference between pure animals and purified or cleansed animals. There is a difference in initial pureness compared with treated, cleansed, or purified animals. For example, a diseased animal may be treated and "cleaned," but it would not qualify. Furthermore, the word holy is translated pure in some passages. Therefore, God is calling for man to recognize and teach that there is a difference between the pure and profane, the sanctified and the sacrilegious.

Similarly, only priests properly sanctified by the temporary shedding and sprinkling of the blood of "clean" (Heb. חהור, tahowr) animals could serve in the sanctuary. The blood of the "clean" animals covered (atoned for) the priests. This was a temporary ordinance until the incarnation of our "clean" Great God and Saviour and the shedding of His blood for our sins. In the New Testament, the covering (sprinkling) of a repentant, saved man by the shed, pure blood of Christ, sanctifies, purifies, sets aside, and causes the priesthood of believers to be declared clean, pure, or holy in the eyes of a Holy God.

We must purpose to show that there is a difference between things man has placed his tool upon (Ex. 20:25, Deut. 27:5) and things that are innately or inherently clean or pure. Translations of the Words of

God are words that have been "tooled" by men. Words declared pure by God in the *received* Hebrew, Aramaic, and Greek texts, which were made available throughout the generations of man for translations, have not been 'tooled' by man (2 Pe. 1:19-21). They are the Words recorded as commanded by God. God said these are "*my words*" (Psa. 56:5, and fifty plus other places)

We are required to show the **difference** between tooled and untooled Words. We are also required to show the **difference** between a truly "pure" man or one purified by the shed blood of the perfect, sinless, clean Lamb of God, who needs no purifying, whose blood covers (atones) us, whose Words wash us, and whose sacrifice on the Cross of Calvary was out of **pure** love.

The Meaning of "Pure" in Scripture Applied to Man

Before examining the meaning of the phrase, *"pure words"* of God, let us look at the Scriptural intent of *"pure"* as applied to man. Matthew 5:8 and 1 Pe. 1:22 encourages man to make every effort to remove guile and hypocrisy in his relationships "*through the Spirit unto unfeigned love of the brethren.*" Nevertheless, he will not be "pure" or "perfect" as the Lord Jesus Christ, because man has a "*deceitful*" and "*desperately wicked*" heart. The last phrase of 1 Peter 1:22 and the next verse clarify the meaning of a *"pure heart,"* saying:

> "*see that ye love one another with **a pure heart** fervently: **Being born again**, not of corruptible seed, but of incorruptible, by the word of God, which liveth and abideth for ever*" (1 Peter 1:22-23).

So what does Peter mean when he exhorts believers to *"see that ye love one another with a pure heart fervently"* (1 Pe. 1:22)? The answer follows in verse twenty-three: ***"Being born again."***

The point of these verses is to remind us of the indwelling of the Holy Spirit, the Lord Jesus Christ, and the Father, who are the *"pure heart"* within us, in spite of the continued presence of the *"old man."* When David pleads for God to *"create in me a clean heart"* (Psa. 51:10), *"clean"* is the same Hebrew word used for "pure" in many verses and implies the purifying or cleansing of our spirit, soul, and body. Of course for the mature believer this is accomplished by dying daily to **self** on the Cross, and by removing hypocrisy and guile in all of our relationships. In addition, in Old Testament times, the Holy Spirit did not permanently indwell; so it could be interpreted as a plea for the indwelling of the Holy Spirit.

The heart of man is dirty, sinful, deceitful, and wicked. A discerning man cries out for God to cleanse him and to provide the power to live a Christian life. How is this possible? It should no longer be man's heart that controls a born-again man, but the Spirit of God, the Lord Jesus Christ, the Father, and their Words which dwell within our hearts to provide power over the flesh (Jn. 14:17, 23, Rom. 1:4, 8:9, 1 Cor. 1:24, 2 Cor. 6:16, Eph. 1:13, 3:17, Col. 3:16, 2 Tim. 1:7, Jas. 4:5).

Another verse proclaims, *"every man that hath this hope in him purifieth himself, even as he is pure"* (1 John 3:3). Every man who looks for His appearing strives to follow the character, personality, morality, and virtue of the Lord Jesus Christ; *"he strives now to be pure as Christ is pure."*[11] He strives to purify his life, actions, thoughts, attitudes, and

---

[11] Rev. Justin Edwards, D.D. and Rev. Prof. E. P. Harrows, D.D, *The Family Bible, Containing the Old and New Testament, With Brief Notes and Instructions* (SwordSearcher, Version 5.1.1.1, Broken Arrow, OK, 2007, The Family Bible Notes were first published 1861) Comments on 1 John 3:3.

relationships by the washing of the Word and the power available to him. Certainly, the purifying cannot and will not occur through man, who walks after the flesh and not after the Spirit. The Holy Spirit is the power, righteousness, purity, wisdom, understanding, discernment, and holiness of God. He is the gift of God who dwells in a regenerated man. In a born-again man, the Holy Spirit is the provider of gifts and power (Rom. 8:1ff, 15:13, 19, 1 Cor. 12:4-7, 2 Cor. 1:22, Eph. 1:13).

Natural man, who does not have a *"pure heart"* by virtue of the indwelling of God, has a choice to believe or not to believe. If man believes in the Lord Jesus Christ, he is regenerated. After salvation, a man also has a choice whether or not to allow God's power to overcome the flesh.

To God Be the Glory

A significant problem is interfering with these concepts in this present age. It has to do with the exaltation of self by the tenets of modern and postmodern psychology and psychiatry. It is beyond the scope of this work to elucidate the difficulties, but everyone should be aware of the anti-Biblical stand of these modern professions, which are non-scientific, humanistic philosophies. A born-again man exalting himself will grieve the Holy Spirit, who desires to empower a believer, but not by force. In addition, God will give his glory to no one else, especially someone exalting himself (Isa. 42:8, 11, Rev. 4:11). God's plea with man is to abandon self and to be guided by His Words and the power of the Holy Spirit (Rom. 8:1-10, Psa. 25:9, 32:8, 109:105).

A Pure Man Has the Life of God Infused

The great preacher C. H. Spurgeon indicates how it is possible for man to be pure and to walk after the Spirit:

"The life of God infused in regeneration is as **pure** as the Lord by whom it was begotten, and can never be otherwise. Blessed is the man who has this heavenly principle within, for it must appear in his life, and cause him to abound in holiness, to the glory of God."[12] (my emphasis, HDW).

A man may abound in holiness, but to declare that he is "pure" is contrary to Scripture. It is more appropriate to call someone a believer or born-again than to call him pure. Albert Barnes relates the responsibility of each believer to set himself aside to strive for the perfection in Christ by yielding to the Spirit, which will not be perfectly reached until he is translated. Commenting on 1 John 3:3, Barnes said:

"That is, under the influence of this hope of being like the Saviour, he puts forth those efforts in struggling against sin, and in overcoming his evil propensities, which are necessary to make him pure. The apostle would not deny that for the success of these efforts we are dependent on Divine aid; but he brings into view, as is often done in the sacred writings, the agency of man himself as essentially connected with success. Comp. Php 2:12. The particular thought here is, that the hope of being like Christ, and of being permitted to dwell with him, will lead a man to earnest efforts to become holy, and will be actually followed by such a result.

"Even as he is pure." The same kind of purity here, the same degree hereafter. That is, the tendency of such a hope is to make him holy now, though he may be imperfect; the effect will be to make him perfectly holy in the world to come. It cannot be shown from this passage that the apostle meant to teach that any one actually becomes as pure in the present life as the Saviour is, that is, becomes perfectly holy; for all that is fairly implied in it is, that those who have this hope in them *aim* at the same purity, and will *ultimately* obtain it. But the apostle does not say that it is attained in

[12] C. H. Spurgeon, *Flowers From a Puritan's Garden* (Sprinkle Publications, Harrisonburg, VA, 1997) 14.

this world. If the passage *did* teach this, it would teach it respecting every one who has this hope, and then the doctrine would be that no one can be a Christian who does not become absolutely perfect on earth; that is, not that some Christians may become perfect here, but that all actually *do*. But none, it is presumed, will hold this to be a true doctrine. A true Christian does not, indeed, habitually and willfully sin; but no one can pretend that all Christians attain to a state of sinless perfection on earth, or are, in fact, as pure as the Saviour was. But unless the passage proves that *every* Christian becomes absolutely perfect in the present life, it does not prove that in fact any do. It proves

(1.) that the tendency, or the fair influence of this hope, is to make the Christian pure;

(2.) that all who cherish it will, in fact, aim to become as holy as the Saviour was; and

(3.) that this object will, at some future period, be accomplished. There is a world where all who are redeemed shall be perfectly holy."[13]

Therefore, the believer must take up his cross daily and follow Christ because the believer is not personally perfectly pure. He must die daily on his cross to self (Lk. 9:23). He must follow Paul's declaration in Gal. 2:20. We must yield our lives by faith daily and moment by moment to the perfect God who dwells within, because the "old man," which is the flesh, is weak and will lead us astray (cf. Gal. 6:14, Rom. 8:1ff.). Like Paul, we must realize:

> *"Not as though I had already attained, either were already perfect: but I follow after, if that I may apprehend that for which also I am apprehended of Christ Jesus"* (Philippians 3:12).

---

[13] Albert Barnes, *Albert Barnes' Notes on the Bible* (SwordSearcher, Broken Arrow, OK, 2007, originally published 1832-1872) comments on 1 Jn. 3:3.

And yet, we strive to be like the Lord Jesus Christ; we strive to not sin, to honor and serve our Lord, and to be His ambassadors just as Paul declared:

> *"What shall we say then? Shall we continue in sin, that grace may abound? God forbid. How shall we, that are dead to sin, live any longer therein?"* (Romans 6:1-2).

In conclusion, we dare not call man "pure;" it is the life within us that is perfectly pure. Rather, we **strive** to be pure. It is risky to call any man pure, because some may believe that they are sinless. Perhaps it is best to declare a believer good, or born-again, or a man or woman of God. The Scripture calls a man pure who is walking in the Spirit by virtue of God's power and not by the virtue of his own flesh.

What Does "Pure" Word(s) of God Mean?

What is meant by *"pure"* when we speak of the Words of God? Does it mean accurate and faithful words chosen by men who translate the Words of God? Are the "pure" Words the original language *received* Hebrew/Aramaic/Greek Words? Are the "pure" Words those constructed by textual critics such as Tischendorf, Bengal, Westcott, Hort, and others, which are texts generally known as the UBS/NA *critical texts*?

Obviously, there are perfect and pure Words, which cannot be changed, added to, or subtracted from. The Scripture indicates very clearly that there are "certain" pure Words of truth (Pro. 22:21). There are Words that cannot be corrupted because the Lord Himself will watch over them (Psa. 12:6-7, 138:2) There are Words which God warns man not to corrupt (Deut. 4:2, Pro. 30:5-6, Rev. 22:18-19). Where are these pure Words?

What do men mean when they say the King James Bible is *"pure"*? Do they mean there is no dependency on the underlying original language Words? Do they mean there is no **difference** in purity from the underlying original language Words (Eze. 22:26)? Do they mean the words are wholly separate, inspired, perfect, pure and given by God?

Men make similar statements about the inspiration of the Words of God as they do about the purity of God's Words. For example, a good brother and faithful evangelist said the following about the King James Bible:

> "It amazes me that even in Christian circles there are so many who in one way or another dilute and diminish the text of Scripture. **They simply cannot bring themselves to say that we have an inspired text preserved for us in the English language**...I can't imagine going to the pulpit to preach without the assurance that the Book I hold in my hands is, in fact, the literal Word of Almighty God, **inspired**, preserved and our full complete authority." (SOL, Editorial, Oct. 5, 2007)

Just as preservation and inspiration go hand-in-hand, purity and inspiration go hand-in-hand. Therefore, can we call any text inspired of God or the "pure" Words of God? God declares that we must show the **difference** between the pure and unclean (Eze. 22:26). Although the King James Bible is the most incredible English literary work ever to be produced, is it pure and inspired like the original Words recorded by the Apostles and prophets of God? The King James Bible is an incredible work primarily because **it is based upon** the pure, inspired, inerrant, infallible Words of God. However, that does not mean that it obtains a derivative inspiration or purity that God attributes to His foundational Words in the original languages of the Bible (see the Preface to this work). They are the foundation that is preserved to the jot and tittle, which also means the word order and spelling. The King James Bible has already had many spelling changes, but NONE of God's original Words have been changed, although the attacks on them have been ferocious. The King James Bible is a verbally plenarily translated Bible (VPT).

Can all of the accurate and faithful Words (VPT) of the King James Bible be understood perfectly without the need to consult the grammar of the original Words? Have the words in the King James Bible changed, as the spelling was modernized or as minor printing corrections were made?

The spellings of the original Words in Hebrew/Aramaic/Greek given by God are the precise, pure "letters" (jots and tittles). We can say without hesitation that they are verbally plenarily preserved and inspired (VPP and VPI). Dean John William Burgon[14] (1813-1888), Dean of Chichester, spent many hours tracking down one letter in one word because God promised their preservation and warned anyone not to make a change in them (Deut. 4:1-2, Pro. 30:5-6, Rev. 22:18-19).

Some men believe the accurate and faithful words of the King James Bible are pure like the original Words (see below). But the spelling of the words has changed; whereas God's original Words do not change in spelling or in word order. There have been no deletions nor additions to them. Spurgeon understood that the pure Words of God were the Words given by God, which were without "flaw" or "error." He said:

---

[14] "John William Burgon (1813 -1888) was a man of tremendous intellect and ranks among men such a Lancelot Andrews (1555 -1626) and Robert Dick Wilson (1856 -1930) in scholarship. He became the Dean of Chichester and has since been known as "Dean" Burgon. Dr. Burgon was contemporary with Westcott and Hort. He was an advocate of the Textus Receptus and was the nemesis of Westcott and Hort's feeble arguments against it. He believed, unlike Westcott and Hort, in basing all conclusions on the solid foundation of facts rather than the sand of theory. He would leave no stone unturned in his quest for truth and no blow undelivered in his defense of it." (from www.deanburgonsociety.org/#Who%20Was).

"This Bible is a book of authority; it is an authorized book, for God has written it. Oh! tremble, lest any of you despise it; mark its authority, for it is the Word of God. Then, since God wrote it, mark *its truthfulness.* If I had written it, there would be worms of critics who would at once swarm upon it, and would cover it with their evil spawn; Had I written it, there would be men who would pull it to pieces at once, and perhaps quite right too. But this is the Word of God; come, search, ye critics, and **find a flaw**; examine it, from its Genesis to its Revelation, and **find an error**. **This is a vein of pure gold**, unalloyed by quartz, or any earthly substance."[15]

Even the KJB translators understood the words that they chose were an attempt by man to do the best he could translating the original unchanging Words (VPT).[16] So, what do men mean when they call the KJB *"pure"*? For example:

"We teach and preach only from the **pure** word of God—the King James Bible. Our choice of a Bible version is based upon conviction as well as history. Conviction in that we believe God promised to preserve His word (Psalm 12:6-7) and history in that the Bible we use contains the very same verses that have been used by churches since God completed His word in the First Century A.D. Our theme verse is Psalm 128:2b, "Thou hast magnified thy word above all thy name."[17]

Our good brother, Dr. David Cloud, calls the King James Bible "pure."

"The material in this volume is given from an unapologetically Bible-believing position. We make no apology for the Word of God, and we refuse to question any

---

[15] Spurgeon, op. cit., 104 (Sermon 1).
[16] King James Bible, 1611, Preface, "To the Readers."
[17] Pastor George Shafer, "We preach only from the pure word of God" http://www.odentonbaptist.org/?q=node/2. Accessed 10/11/07. Compare similar statements at http://www.baptistpillar.com/bd0407.htm

of its statements. We also believe we have a **pure** Bible in the King James translation of the Received Text."[18]

In Dr. Cloud's book, *Things Hard to be Understood,* he quotes *"The Second London Confession"* of 1677, which speaks of the inspired written Word of God, and says:

"If the Bible is undependable in its science, it is certainly not what it claims to be, which is the **pure** Word of God."[19]

The section where this statement is located seems to apply to the *received* Hebrew/Aramaic/Greek Words. He proceeds to discuss the dependability of the King James Bible in the next section, but does not call it pure or inspired.

For some of us, it is a contradiction to call the original language Words of the Bible pure and to follow that claim by calling **any** translation pure. Why? Not every Bible text that man claims to be pure can be truly pure. Saints need to consider what texts they are going to call pure, just as they should consider what texts they call inspired. Not every text can be inspired. Not every text can be pure. What follows in this work are some of the concepts believers must understand to sharpen the definitions and use of the words *"pure"* and *"inspiration."*

For example, some individuals are claiming that the 'new' modern versions, which are translations of several corrupted texts by dynamic equivalent translating (DET), are true and pure. A quote on an internet site about the *"pure"* 'word of God' was discovered that seems to combine

---

[18] David Cloud, *Way of Life Encyclopedia* (Way of Life Literature, Port Huron, MI, SwordSearcher Module, 2007) Under the section: 1_ How To Use This Bible Encyclopedia.

[19] David Cloud, *Things Hard to be Understood* (Way of Life Literature, Port Huron, MI, 1996) 12.

two phrases from two different translations into one verse; one of the phrases is from the NIV and the other is from the NLT:

> "The Bible says:
>   'Every word of God proves true (**NLT**); he is a shield to those who take refuge in him (**NIV**).' Proverbs 30:5
>   And that's a powerful truth that time and eternity both bear witness to."[20] (my addition of version and emphasis in parentheses, HDW)

The author of this same site believes the "message" by **any** translation is satisfactory, saying:

> "I am convinced that the Bible translation is not so important as the heart and mind of the man or woman of God. We can read the simplest and easiest translation of the Bible, but if our hearts are not listening to the Lord, we won't get the **message**. On the other hand, when the heart is ready to hear from God, **any Bible will do**."[21] (my emphasis, HDW).

Others claim that **all** the Words of the Bible are not pure. For example, the following chart was found on another website:

Is Every Word of God Pure[22]	
YES	**NO**
Psalm 2:6 The words of the LORD are pure words: as silver tried in a furnace of earth, purified seven times. Psalm 119:140 Thy word is very pure: therefore thy servant loveth	2 Kings 18:27 Hath he not sent me to the mean which sit on the wall, that they may eat their own dung, and drink their own piss with you? Ezekiel 23:20 For she doted upon their paramours, whose flesh is as the

---

[20] Jim Sutton, "Every Word of God Proves True" (http://www.goodwordusa.org/word/pure.htm). Accessed 10/11/07.
[21] Ibid. http://www.goodwordusa.org/power/bibles.htm.
[22] http://skepticsannotatedbible.com/contra/pure.html

it.
Proverbs 30:5
    Every word of God is pure.
	flesh of asses, and whose issue is like the issue of horses.
	Habakkuk 2:16
	    Drink thou also, and let thy foreskin be uncovered.
	Malachi 2:3
	    Behold, I will corrupt your seed, and spread dung upon your faces.

God did not say, **"some"** of the Words of God are *"pure"*; as a matter of fact, He said *"every word"* (Prov. 30:5, cf. Psa. 12:6,). So, we must ask, "Where are the *"pure"* Words of God?" and "How can the words in any text, any Bible or any translation be "pure," "truth," "preserved," "precise," "inerrant," "infallible," "inspired" and *"the voice of the Words of God,"* since there are many Bibles with different words and different messages? Obviously, they cannot all be "pure." However, the person claiming the words in the chart above are not pure Words obviously lacks even the basic knowledge of the Scripture. The Words are perfect. The Words may seem evil, but the Old Testament serves as an example and as a warning for believers in this age (1 Cor. 10:6).

A Firm Definition of "Pure" Must Be Established

Believers must draw 'a line in the sand' somewhere, or else every word of man, every action by man, every philosophy by man, every poem by man, etc. will be called "pure." Any thinking student will obviously be offended and astounded at men who use the words "pure" "inspired," and "inerrant" without discernment and care. Pure means without contamination of **any** sort, or without the need for **any** further refining, or without **any** corruption.[23] A 'standard' must be established for which Words are called "*pure.*" Where are we to draw the line? Did God indicate which Words we were to "*receive*" and "*keep*" as "pure" and as the foundation for translations (Psa. 11:3, Pro. 2:1, Eze. 3:10, Jn. 14:23)? He did, and His Words declare that "*every word of God is pure*" and "*his way is perfect: the word of God is tried*" (Pro. 30:5, Psa. 18:30).

In the past, many men have considered that their words were just as "*pure*" and "*inspired*" as the Bible. For example, Samuel T. Coleridge, who wrote *Kubla Khan*, who had a great influence on the Broad Church Movement in England, and who influenced Westcott and Hort, believed his words were equivalent to Scripture. He said they were as inspired as the Psalms written by David.[24]

God repeatedly declares in the Scriptures, "***my words***" (Nu. 12:6, Deut. 4:10, 11:18, Isa. 51:16, Jer. 1:9, etc.). He declares:

> "*Heaven and earth shall pass away, but **my words** shall not pass away*" (Matthew 24:35) "*Heaven and earth shall pass away: but **my words** shall not pass away*" (Mark 13:31)."*Heaven and earth shall pass away: but **my words** shall not pass away*" (Luke 21:33).

Believers in the Lord Jesus Christ must come to the realization that their claims, ideas, thoughts, philosophies, words, etc., are not God's thoughts or ways or **Words** (Isa. 55:7-11, Jer. 10:23). Our Maker gave us specific, precise Words, which He said would be (and are) VPI and VPP (Psa. 12:6-7, Prov. 30:5-6, Mat. 4:4, 5:17-18, Jn. 10:35, 2 Tim. 3:15-16). But where are the "*pure*" Words and where is the accurate and faithful translation of the Words? Are they preserved in Hebrew, Aramaic, and

---

[23] See *The 1828 Webster Dictionary* definition in the chart, "Hebrew, Aramaic, Greek, English Words Related to Pure," at the end of this work.
[24] H. D. Williams, M.D., Ph.D., *The Lie That Changed The Modern World* (Bible For Today Press, Collingswood, NJ, 2004) 59-60.

Greek, or in Gothic, English, Coptic, French, German, Spanish, etc.? Are they in the different editions of the *Received Texts*? Are they in the constructed 27th edition of the United Bible Society Text (UBS)? The apostate professors, Westcott and Hort (WH), produced the text the UBS and the Nestle Aland texts follow.

There are competing original Biblical language texts in Hebrew, Aramaic, and Greek that are purported to be the Word(s) of God. There are texts of the Greek New Testament that differ by at least 8,000 words; much less, texts and versions of the Old Testament. Dr. D. A. Waite reports demonstrate that in the footnotes of the Biblia Hebraica, there are suggested some 20,000 to 30,000 in the Hebrew text..[25] There are competing translations with very different words that are alleged to be the "pure" word of God. How can all of these "works" that are so different be the "pure words of God"? If the words are changed, the message is changed. If the translation of the Word(s) of God is **not** accurate and faithful the message will be compromised.

> "Words form thoughts, messages, ideas, and content. They are the building blocks of communications. Words determine the message, not the message, the words. Therefore, the words, and even the word order, in a language are important. Dr. Leland Ryken, [who is the] Clyde S. Kilby Professor of English at Wheaton College and author of many books, said:

---

[25] See these works, Dr. Jack Moorman, *8,000 Difference Between the Textus Receptus and the Nestle-Aland NT Greek Texts* (Bible For Today Press and Dean Burgon Society Press, Collingswood, NJ, 2007) and Dr. D. A. Waite, Th.D., Ph.D., *The New International Version, Weighed In The Balance—And Found Wanting, The N.I.V. Is Not The Word of God In English* (Bible For Today Press, Collingswood, NJ, 1990).

> "There is no meaning without words, if we change the words, we change the meaning."[26]

This means that *"one jot or one tittle"* (Matthew 5:18) has 'significance' in a word, and meaning is lost if the word is changed in *any* way. For example, if a singular word is changed to a plural word, the theological implication and meaning could be very significantly affected (cf. Galatians 3:16)."[27] [my addition for clarity, HDW]

Martin Luther recognized the importance of words, and therefore, having the God-breathed Words, saying in response to John 6:63:

> "Christ did not say of His thoughts, but of His words, that they are spirit and life."[28]

Augustine (354-430 A.D.) recognized that the Scripture is best designated as the pure Words of God and not pure Word of God. The message of Scripture is made from pure Words, "like silver purged from its dross," which are given from heaven to be recorded by men. Augustine said:

> "Then [in this new life] man, made perfect and at rest, purified in body and in soul by **the pure words of God**, which are **like silver purged from its dross**, seven times refined..."[29]

---

[26] J. L. Packer et al, *Translating Truth, The Case For Essentially Literal Bible Translation* (Crossway Books, Wheaton, IL, 2005) 69.

[27] H. D. Williams, M.D., Ph.D., *Word-For-Word Translating the Received Texts, Verbal Plenary Translating* (Bible For Today Press, Collingswood, NJ, 2007) 44.

[28] Wayne Gruden, LeLand Ryken, C. Hohn Collins, Vern S. Poythress, Bruce Winter, *Translating Truth, The Case for Essentially Literal Bible Translation (Crossway Books, Wheaton, IL, 2005)* 60. Martin Luther is quoted.

[29] Augustine, "Questions of Januarius" (*The Nicene and Post Nicene Fathers*, Letters of St. Augustine, Letter 55, The Master Christian Library, Ages Librarian, Ver. 8, 2000) 600.

If words are changing in texts and translations, the meaning must change. If the words are changed, the message must change. **If words are changed, which words are "pure"**? Surely, **any** word, words, or message cannot be pure; in this evil time, it is important to identify which words are stable, pure, and properly translated. Surely, original Biblical language texts with many differing words all claiming to be true, pure, perfect, precise, etc., cannot all be Truth. It does not make sense to believe that any text is pure or any translated text is *"pure."* Only His Words are *"pure."*

God replies to the questions above in Scripture. Only **His Words** are *"pure."* He will speak to other nations, people, and language-groups through translations, but the "standard" or "foundation" is fixed, preserved, and watched over by Him (Isa. 49:22, 59:19, 62:10, Jer. 50:2, Psa. 11:3). His people are required to study and learn **His** counsel, which will stand forever, in order to carry out His commandments through the assistance of pastors/teachers with accurate and faithful translations (Rom. 16:25-26, Eph. 4:11). For example, consider the following few verses among many verses which declare His Words will be present forever, and we are to be careful not to trust in *"lying words;"* rather trust in *"the scriptures of the prophets"* (Rom. 16:26) and Apostles (Eph. 2:20):

> *"Declaring the end from the beginning, and from ancient times the things that are not yet done, saying, **My counsel shall stand**, and I will do all my pleasure"* (Isaiah 46:10).
> *"Behold, ye trust in **lying words**, that cannot profit"* (Jeremiah 7:8).
> *"Therefore thou shalt speak **all these words** unto them; but they will not hearken to thee: thou shalt also call unto them; but they will not answer thee"* (Jeremiah 7:27).
> *"The prophet that hath a dream, let him tell a dream; and he that hath my word, let him speak **my word** faithfully." What is the chaff to the wheat? saith the LORD"*
> *Is not **my word** like as a fire? saith the LORD; and like a*

hammer that breaketh the rock in pieces?" (Jeremiah 23:28-29).

*"Therefore, behold, I am against the prophets, saith the LORD, that steal **my words** every one from his neighbour"* (Jeremiah 23:30).

*"Behold, the days come, saith the Lord GOD, that I will send a famine in the land, not a famine of bread, nor a thirst for water, but of hearing **the words of the LORD**: And they shall wander from sea to sea, and from the north even to the east, they shall run to and fro to seek the word of the LORD, and shall not find it"* (Amos 8:11-12).

*"But he answered and said, It is written, Man shall not live by bread alone, but by **every word** that proceedeth out of the mouth of God"* (Matthew 4:4).

*"But all this was done, that **the scriptures of the prophets** might be fulfilled. Then all the disciples forsook him, and fled."* (Matthew 26:56).

Have you fled from the Truth?

Matthew 4:4 is very apropos to this discussion. Dr. Thomas Strouse, Dean of Emmanuel Baptist Theological Seminary, makes the following comments on Matthew 4:4 about the bibliology of the Lord:

> This response (Mat. 4:4) summarizes the Lord's bibliology. **1)** He affirms the doctrine of the verbal, plenary inspiration of the *autographa* by stating the source of Scripture—"the mouth of God." **2)** He affirms the authority of Scripture, and consequently its infallibility and inerrancy, by upholding it as a **standard** by which "man shall live." **3)** He affirmed the doctrine of the verbal, plenary preservation of Scripture by the expression "It is written" (Gegraptai). The perfect tense which He utilized expresses a completed action with the resulting state of being. In effect, the Lord said "It was written and still is written." The Living Word (Christ) validated **His written Words** since He believed He had the verbal, plenary **preserved** *OT* Words intact in His day.[30] (my emphasis, HDW).

---

[30] Thomas M. Strouse , *"But My Words Shall Not Pass Away" The Biblical Defense of the Doctrine of the Preservation of Scripture* (Emmanuel Baptist Theological Press, Newington, CT, 2001) 12.

Were God's original Words written in English, Spanish, German, Latin, Gothic, Coptic, etc.?[31] Of course not. However, we must have the "pure" verbal plenary inspired Words of God as He promised or God is a liar.

> *"...the gospel of God (Which he had promised afore by his prophets in the **holy** (ἁγίαις) scriptures)"* (Romans 1:1c-2) [my addition, HDW].

One should note that the Greek word, ἁγὶος (hagios), often translated holy, is also translated *"pure."* Try substituting "pure" in these verses: Lk. 1:72, 2 Pe. 2:21, Jude 1:20, 2 Tim. 1:9, 1 Pe. 1:15, 2 Pe. 3:11. Our conversation and behavior should be holy; that is, following His pure Words. His *"holy commandment delivered"* **only** *"once"* refers to His Holy (pure) Words, which are the foundation of our faith (2 Pe. 2:21, Jude 1:3). Please note that the Lord's bibliology concerning His inscripturated "pure" Words, which are *"for ever...settled in heaven,"* which were recorded by His prophets and Apostles, and which were and are preserved by sanctified churches, extends to the **Words** of the New Testament (cf. Mat. 24:35, 1 Pe. 1:23-25, 2 Pe. 3:15-16, 1 Tim. 3:15-16, etc.).

Jesus Declared the Pure, Preserved Words

Jesus repeatedly indicated that He was using the Holy (pure) Words of the Old Testament by declaring: *"It is written"* (e.g. Mat. 4:4, 7, 11, 21:13, 26:31, etc.) *"It is written"* occurs 67 times in the New Testament. Jesus indicated that not one jot or tittle would disappear from the law (Mat. 5:17-18). He quoted a Psalm and indicated it was part of the law (Jn. 10:34-35). He was indicating the Psalms were on an equal basis to "the

---

[31] Verbal plenary translation by the translators for the French Ostervald Bible was recently confirmed. Is it inspired? (See the Dean Burgon Society website, http://biblefortoday.org/idx_foreign_bibles.htm)

Law of Moses" called the Pentateuch. He frequently referred to the law, prophets, and Psalms to indicate all of the Holy Words of Scripture. He declared: *"Heaven and earth shall pass away, but my words shall not pass away"* (Matthew 24:35). He declared the Scripture cannot be *"broken,"* meaning destroyed (Jn. 10:35, cf. Mat. 5:19). When He made this declaration, He had "certain" Words already written in His mind; the thirty-nine books of the Canon of the Old Testament. His Apostles and prophets recorded more of His Words, which became the twenty-seven books of the New Testament, containing many proofs that they are the VPI and VPP Words. The sixty-six books of the Canon of Scripture are the pure Words and they are "foundation" for the work of translating work into the languages of the world.

It is dangerous to extend our use of the word holy (pure) to words spoken or chosen by men, even though our Lord commanded that His Words be made available to other nations in their language (Jer. 23:28-29, Mat. 28:20, Rom. 16:25-27, 1 Cor. 14:21). This could be compared to His command for His saints to "go into the world and preach the gospel to every creature (Mk. 16:15). He sends regenerated men who are not pure like Him or His Words to do the job He intends. The men are not perfect, but purified by the indwelling perfect, pure God. Likewise, the accurate and faithful translations of the pure, original Words have imputed authority (see the preface of this work).

As many researchers have discovered through examination of the 'new' versions, men's words may be corrupting. The words are often either DETs or based upon corrupted texts; or both. They reject many of the *received* VPI Words promised and preserved through the nation Israel and the sanctified churches. Furthermore, far too often in these last days, men are accepting the words of scholars who are so often independent of oversight by one of God's assemblies. They add their own impure words to the counsel of wisdom by scholarship rather than *receiving* by faith the Words available from generation to generation. Gregory of Nyssa (d. 385 or 386 A.D.) said:

> "Would it not have been safer for all, following the counsel of wisdom... in peace and quietness to keep inviolate **the pure deposit of the faith**?"[32]

How Some Use the Word Pure

This subject is important for us today because many things are called pure, which may not be pure; they may be faithful, accurate, cleaned or repaired, but not pure in the sense of the "pure" inscripturated Words of God and the incarnate Son of God. Some individuals use the word pure to refer to words in several differing Bible texts: either the *Critical Texts* such as the UBS/NA texts or the *Traditional/Received Texts* (TT/RT). Others call versions or DETs and AFTs of the Bible pure.

Remember, God calls the Words "pure," which have been available to all generations as they were revealed and which were watched over by Him in the institutions charged by Him with the responsibility to "receive" and "keep" them.[33] The only text this author can identify as being available to every generation is the Traditional Texts/Received Texts. Supporting information is available from many sources. It behooves us to identify from Scripture what the Lord considers "pure."

---

[32] Gregory of Nyssa, *Against Eunomius* (The Life and Writings of Gregory of Nyssa, The Nicene and Post Nicene Fathers, The Master Christian Library, Ages Software, 2000) 513.
[33] See the next chapter, "Receiving and Keeping the Words of God."

How the Inscripturated Words of God Use the Word Pure

A study of the use and application of the English word, "*pure*," in the translations of the texts *received* through the sanctified churches reveals an interesting fact. The word "*pure*" is a translation of **many different** Hebrew/Aramaic/Greek Words; in fact, there are seventeen (see the attached chart). They have nuances of meaning that cannot be reflected in the one English word "pure." The ancient Hebrew and Greek speaking people would understand the nuances and differences in the underlying words presently translated by one English word. This also suggests that English-speaking people need to be more selective in their use of the word "pure." This is especially true in light of the predilection of this age to use the word pure to apply to many things that simply are not pure.

This work is an attempt to clarify the use of "pure" in the Scriptures for the English-speaking language groups. The differences are not readily seen without consulting the original "pure" Words given to the Apostles and prophets and preserved through the generations. The differences will have a bearing on (1) which Words are considered inspired, inerrant, infallible, accurate, or faithful and (2) which Words are called "pure" in the same sense that the Son of God is "pure;" never needing to be cleansed or purified.

The Pure Words of the Lord Are Clean Not Cleansed

In Psalm 12:6, the Scripture says, *"The words of the Lord are pure words."* This is a statement of fact. A simile designated by "as" subsequently follows this reality to augment the significance of just how "*pure*" the Words of God are. His Words are "*as*" or 'like' as refiner of silver refined them seven[34] times. The Hebrew word used is חהור (tahowr), which means clean or pure(-ness) in regard to the physical, chemical, ceremonial or moral sense.

In other places, the Bible clearly states that the Words given to the Apostles and prophets were "*pure.*" The Hebrew word, ערף (tsaraph), means they were tried, purged, or refined in heaven "*as silver tried in a furnace of earth, purified seven times*" and "*for ever...settled in heaven.*" These are statements of fact.

> "*Thy word is **very pure**: therefore thy servant loveth it*" (Psalms 119:140). "*Every word of God is **pure**: he is a shield unto them that put their trust in him*" (Proverbs 30:5).

God's Words Are For Ever Settled in Heaven

The Words of God were chosen in eternity past (Psa. 119:89, Isa. 65:6) by the Trinity before they were given to the Apostles and prophets to record (Jn. 16:13, 17:8, Eph. 2:20, 1 Pe. 1:23-25, 2 Pe. 1:20-21, 2 Pe. 3:2). The Words of the Lord were refined and chosen before the foundation of the world (Mat. 13:35, Eph. 1:4, Rev. 13:8). They are "*for ever...settled.*"

They were "*written before*" and are "*before*" Him in heaven "*for ever*" (Psa. 117, 119:89, Isa. 65:6). The angel who explained Daniel's vision of "*things to come,*" noted that he would "*show [Daniel] that which is noted **in the scripture of truth**" present in heaven (Dan. 10:21).

The Words were "*for ever...settled*" in heaven and given to Daniel to record even though He did **not** understand them (Dan. 12:8-9). The

---

[34] Seven is the number for perfection or completeness in Scripture.

Apostle John noted the visions recorded in the book of Revelation were *"until the words of God shall be fulfilled"* (Rev. 17: 17, Jn. 17:17). In other words, the Words of God were recorded in heavenly places and would be fulfilled.

Please note that the message is given through **Words**, which are from the lips of Him who is the *"Ancient of days."* They are recorded in "books" before Him (Dan. 7:9-10).

They are pure Words, which are recorded in heaven *"in the scripture of truth"* by God, who only is pure. They were there prior to being given to His prophets and Apostles. The pure Words in Hebrew, Aramaic, and Greek were not altered or interpreted by God's prophets or Apostles **and then** recorded as the Words of God (2 Pe. 1:19-21). They are the very words *"for ever...settled in heaven."* They are clean and will never need to be cleansed or purified. They were and are Words chosen by an omniscient God in eternity past.

God Knew in Eternity Past His Apostles and Prophets

God knew who would be His Apostles and prophets. God knew what their vocabulary and experience would be before choosing them to record His Words. In the centuries to follow, the Words given to them to record have been faithfully copied and preserved after the pattern established by God (e.g. Deut. 10:2, Jer. 36:2, 22, 23, 28).

The Words of Man Cannot Compare to God's Words

This is in stark contrast to the words of man as described in the verses preceding verse six of Psalm twelve. In these verses, man's words are described by God as originating from a vain double heart, which gives words that are *"flattering"* or *"proud."* Man claims the puny words from his tongue and lips will prevail (Psa. 12:4). God calls them *"lying words"* and words of *"iniquity and deceit."* (Psa. 36:3, Isa. 32:7, Jer. 7:8, 29:23).

God's Words Are Like a Refiner

The Words of the Lord are so pure that *"the voice of his words"* from His lips is described as an agent that is capable of refining and cleaning other things. These Words will act as a *"refiner;"* as a *"judge"* of men now, and at His judgment seat and throne *"in that day"* as final judge of men (Mal. 3:2-3, Jn 12:47-48). God's Words are in no need of being *"cleansed"* or *"purified."*[35] God's Words *"for ever...settled"* do the refining; they do not need to be "refined" or "cleansed" by man, as we shall see. God Himself has refined them in order that the Words are capable of the refining. They are like a refiners *"fire"* and *"like a hammer"*

---

[35] A comment is necessary here. Many men believe that they need to reconstruct the Words of God; they have done exactly that by their construction of texts from a few obviously corrupted texts discarded and refused by the institutions God ordained to preserve His Words. Their "construction" process is far different from the process of collating texts on the basis of seven cardinal principles carefully laid out by men in the past. These principles were intuitively used by the KJB translators as they examined texts and translations and they were enumerated by Dean John William Burgon in several of his books. Isn't it interesting that the KJB translators chose many of the same English Words that Tyndale and the Geneva Bible used for translation because of using the same underlying texts (the RT) and the providential care of God in translation of His "pure" Words? This speaks of virtually identical RT texts and the collating of them in the few places where they differed. The KJB translators make it clear that they translated from the original tongues in their "Preface to the Reader." This is much different from texts and translations that vary significantly in terms of words, doctrinal passages, and other "internal" grammatical changes (i.e. USB/NA texts vary in thousands of places, as do the translations such as NASB, NIV, NLT, RSV, ESV, etc.).

(Jer. 23:29). Similarly and furthermore, the Lord Jesus Christ is in no need of being "*cleansed*" or "*purified.*" He is sinless from the beginning, whether we mean eternity past or from His incarnation and time on earth. He has always been, is, and will be pure. He is the Alpha and Omega, the Aleph and Tav, the beginning and the end, the first and last (Gen. 1:1, Rev. 1:8, 11, 21:6, 22:13). He is the refiner, the refiner's soap, and the refiner's fire (Mal. 3:2-3).

Typology of God's Words and His Son

The *typology* in the Old Testament and the clear statements in the New Testament assure us of the doctrinal truths presented above. For example, a lamb offered as a sacrifice in the Old Testament was "*without blemish,*" typologically like our Savior who was without blemish or sin from the beginning or from eternity (e.g. Nu. 6:14, Eze. 43:22, Jn. 8:46, 9:14). There was no need for the Lamb of God to be purified like other men (1 Jn 3:3). The typology related to these concepts is repeated many times in the Old Testament and in the New Testament. God said He would speak in similitudes, comparisons, or types. This was done for our understanding, as we shall see.

> "*I have also spoken by the prophets, and I have multiplied visions, and used **similitudes**, by the ministry of the prophets*" (Hosea 12:10)

Typology of Gold

Typically, gold is often used as a symbol of purity (e.g. Ex. 25:11, 17, 29, 31, 38, 28:14, 22, 36, 37:4, 11, Mal. 3:3, 1 Cor. 3:12). Even though pure gold is used typologically, it is only a "shadow of the real." It cannot equal the purity of God's "Wisdom"—whether that "Wisdom" represents the Son of God or the Word(s) of God. The Scripture clearly states that Wisdom is valued above *"pure gold"* and *"it cannot be gotten for gold,"* saying:

> *"But where shall wisdom be found? and where is the place of understanding? Man knoweth not the price thereof; neither is it found in the land of the living. The depth saith, It is not in me: and the sea saith, It is not with me. It cannot be **gotten for gold**, neither shall silver be weighed for the price thereof. It **cannot be valued with the gold** of Ophir, with the precious onyx, or the sapphire. The gold and the crystal cannot equal it: and the exchange of it shall not be for jewels of fine gold. No mention shall be made of coral, or of pearls: for the price of wisdom is above rubies. The topaz of Ethiopia shall not equal it, neither shall it be **valued with pure gold**"* (Job 28:12-19).

The Lord Jesus Christ is God's pure Wisdom (Pro. 8, 1 Cor. 1:24, 30). So, typically God's pure Words and God's pure Son are represented by pure gold, yet, even it cannot compare to the true purity of His Words or His Son (Psa. 12:6, Jn. 1:1, 14). If pure gold cannot adequately represent His pure Words, surely then, man needs to place a difference between translated Words compared with the original Words. His preserved original language Words are His pure Words and they are the inspired Words of revelation that are used for translating and for reference. If a question arises in an AFT, the original language Words are consulted in an attempt to resolve the question. This has always been the position of the Dean Burgon Society (DBS). The "Articles of Faith" of the DBS, Section II A, states:

> "We, believe that the King James Version (or Authorized Version) of the English Bible is a true, faithful, and accurate translation of these two providentially preserved Texts (the Hebrew Masoretic Text and Greek Traditional/Received Text), which in our time has no equal among all of the other English Translations. The translators

did such a fine job in their translation task that we can without apology hold up the Authorized Version of 1611 and say "This is the WORD OF GOD!" while at the same time realizing that, in some verses, **we must go back to the underlying original language Texts for complete clarity, and also compare Scripture with Scripture.**"[36] (my addition for clarity, HDW).

Obviously, gold is not pure until refined; so, it is 'made' pure by refining (Heb. וגר cagar = deliver up, repair, 1 Kg 7:49, 50, 1 Kg. 10:21, Mal. 3:3, etc.). The gold ore "delivers up" the pure gold by the refining process. The Words of God were "delivered up" in heaven by God as already pure. In Scripture therefore, refined gold is often used typologically as a forerunner of the truly pure Son of God, who is the Word of God, and as a type of the Words of God.

Many items, implements, or articles in Moses' tabernacle in the wilderness were covered with gold in recognition of this typology. For example, the *"shittim"* wood boards for the walls of the Holy of Holies and Holy Place were covered with *"pure gold"* (Ex 26:29, 2 Ch. 3:4); the candlesticks were *"pure gold"* (Ex. 25:31); the ark of the covenant and the mercy seat were *"pure gold"* (Ex 25:10-11, 17); *"the snuffers, and the basons, and the spoons, and the censers, of pure gold: and the entry of the house, the inner doors thereof for the most holy place, and the doors of the house of the temple, were of gold"* (2 Ch. 22); etc. The twelve cakes of shewbread, which were a type of the Words of God (His commandments, precepts, judgments, or law for the twelve tribes), were placed upon a table of *"pure gold"* (2 Ch. 13:11). In his recorded sermons, C. H. Spurgeon repeatedly confirms his belief in the **unadulterated**, pure Words of God. He said:

---

[36] Dean Burgon Society, "Articles of Faith, Operation, and Organization" (http://www.deanburgonsociety.org/DBS_Society/articles.htm).

This is the book untainted by any error; but is **pure, unalloyed, perfect truth**. Why? Because God wrote it. Ah! charge God with error if ye please; tell him that his book is not what it ought to be. I have heard men, with prudish and mock-modesty, who would like to alter the Bible; and (I almost blush to say it) I have heard ministers **alter** God's Bible, because they were afraid of it. Have you never heard a man say, "He that believeth and is baptized, shall be saved; but he that believeth not" — what does the Bible say? — "Shall be *damned*." But that does not happen to be polite enough, so they say, "Shall be *condemned*."[37]

"*Every word of God*," which we must "*live by*" and "*eat*," is much purer than typological "*pure gold*" (Psa. 12:6, Mat. 4:4). Psalm nineteen confirms this fact:

> "The **statutes** of the LORD are right, rejoicing the heart: the commandment of the LORD is **pure**, enlightening the eyes. The **fear of the LORD** is clean, enduring for ever: the **judgments** of the LORD are true and righteous altogether. **More to be desired are they than gold, yea, than much fine gold**: sweeter also than honey and the honeycomb" (Psalms 19:8-10).

"*Fine*" is from the Hebrew word, פז (paz), which is translated "*pure gold*" as in refined gold in other passages (e.g. Psa 21:3). Obviously, we cannot "*live by*" and "*eat*" His original Words in Hebrew, Aramaic, and Greek if we are not fluent in those languages. We must have translations of them that are as accurate and faithful as possible. They will not be the "*pure*" Words given to the Apostles and prophets, but, if translated according to the model given in Scripture,[38] they will be as

---

[37] C. H. Spurgeon, "The Bible—Sermon 15" (*The Spurgeon Sermon Collection*, The Master Christian Library, Ages Software, 2000) 104.

[38] See the following works for a description of proper translating: H. D. Williams, M.D., Ph.D., *Word-For-Word Translating the Received Texts, Verbal Plenary Translating* (Bible For Today Press, Collingswood, NJ, 2007) and Dr. Thomas Strouse, "The Translation Model Predicted From Scripture"

precise, truthful, correct, sufficient, faithful, and accurate as humanly possible. The translation made by translators could then be considered the preserved Words of God in Spanish, English, French, and other languages. Our Lord commanded the church to make His inspired, preserved Words available in other languages (Matthew 28:19-20, Rom. 16:25-27, 1 Cor. 14:21, Jer. 23:28-29).

Many shepherds fail to understand and appropriate the warnings given to them by God throughout the Scriptures to be certain that His flock, or His sheep, are not fed on words that have been fouled, corrupted, and trampled; that is, words that have been rendered impure. For example, in the book of Isaiah, God has harsh criticism "*against the shepherds of Israel*" concerning these very issues. In chapter 34 of Ezekiel, He concludes a long treatise concerning "*shepherds*" and their failed responsibilities over His flock, or His sheep, with these words:

> "*Seemeth it a small thing unto you to have eaten up the good pasture, but ye must tread down with your feet the residue of your pastures? and to have drunk of the deep waters, but ye must foul the residue with your feet? And as for my flock, they eat that which ye have trodden with your feet; and they drink that which ye have fouled with your feet.*"
> (Ezekiel 34:18-19).

Please do not miss the types in this passage, which refer to God's pure Words that have been fouled by the shepherds who have failed to feed God's flock upon His pure Words. For example, "*the good pasture,*" and "*deep waters*" allude to God's Words which have been trodden or fouled under their feet [cf. Psa. 23:2, 36:6, 92:5, 107:24, Prov. 18:4, Isa. 49:9, 1 Pe. 5:2]. If you are a shepherd, are you "*keeping*" this critical

(Emmanuel Baptist Theological Seminary, Newington, CT, Public Resources on a website, accessed 10/12/07) http://www.emmanuel-newington.org/seminary/resources/KJV_Model.pdf.

duty?[39] How can a man of God, who is fed on *"good pasture(s)"* and who has *"drunk of the deep waters,"* defile the *"clean"* or *"pure"* life-giving Words of God, giving fouled food and drink to those who follow you? This is the very error Westcott and Hort made.

Hopefully, for some of you, one day He will *"sprinkle clean water upon you, and ye shall be clean: from all your filthiness, and from all your idols, will I cleanse you"* (Ezekiel 36:25). The word *"clean"* in the phrase, *"clean water,"* in this verse is from the Hebrew word חהור (tahowr), which is also translated *"pure."* It carries the sense of pure **from the beginning** and is the word used in Psalm 12:6 and Proverbs 30:5 quoted at the beginning of this chapter. The next two words, clean and cleanse in Ezekiel 36:35 are from the Hebrew word חהר (taher), which carries the sense of making something clean or purifying it (cf. Psa. 51:2, Pro. 20:9, Mal. 3:3 where the same Hebrew word is used). Similarly, one day soon, He will purify the church *"that he might sanctify and cleanse it with the washing of water by the word"* (Ephesians 5:26).

Some Similitudes

God has identified His Words by many *"similitudes"* in the Scriptures by which He shall govern the earth and man and by which His shepherds are to feed His people. The "rod," "staff," and "green" or "good pasture" are similitudes for God's Words. For example, *"The LORD'S voice crieth unto the city, and the man of wisdom shall see thy name: hear ye **the rod, and who hath appointed it**"* (Micah 6:9). **"Feed thy people with thy rod, the flock of thine heritage,** *which dwell solitarily in the wood, in the midst of Carmel: let them feed in Bashan*

---

[39] See the Chapter: "Receiving and Keeping the Words of God" for an explanation of "keeping."

and Gilead (the good pasture), as in the days of old" (my addition, HDW) (Micah 7:14, cf. Jer. 6:16). A literal rod cannot speak or feed a flock, but God's Words can. Bashan and Gilead are places of *"good pasture,"* producing strong, fat, nourished cattle (Eze. 39:18, Nu. 32:1, Psa. 22:12). Has your soul delighted *"itself in fatness"* (Isa. 55:2)? Is your flock *"itself in fatness?"*

Other Typologies

Many other typologies in the Old Testament attest to the purity and holiness of God's Son and His Words, which need no cleansing because they are *"without spot"* (Nu. 19:2, 28:3, 11, 17, 1 Tim. 6:14, Heb. 9:14, 1 Pe. 1:19); *"without blemish"* (Ex. 12:5, Lev. 1:3, 21:23, Nu. 6:14, Eze. 43:22, 1 Pe. 1:19); not *"broken"* (Lev. 21:20, Mat. 5:19, Jn. 10:35); *"holy"* (Ex. 30:35, Psa. 138:2, 2 Pe. 2:21). The Lord and His Words are clean from the beginning without any need of refining or reconstruction by textual criticism, a discipline developed by man. The Words were easily collated and confirmed from the manuscripts preserved in the manner and from the path that God chose to preserve them. Dean John William Burgon said:

> "Let us take a slight but comprehensive view of what is found upon investigation, as I hold, to have been **the Divine method** in respect of the New Testament Scriptures...it will be perceived that a three-fold security has been provided for the integrity of the Deposit:—Copies,—Versions,—Fathers. [40]

---

[40] Dean John William Burgon, *The Traditional Text of the Holy Gospels* (Dean Burgon Society Press, Collingswood, NJ, originally published, 1898, 1998) 21, 23.

We have the pure, inspired, preserved, original Words of God. It is interesting to this student of God's Words that the method He chose to preserve them forces our consideration and study of His Words. His Words were passed down and preserved through the centuries in many copies from many regions and in a variety of languages and formats. The research to confirm their preservation has reinforced the fulfillment of God's promise to preserve them.

Pure Saints

Second Samuel twenty-two speaks of David's "cleanness" or "purifying" of himself (2 Sam. 22:21). The Hebrew word used is בר, bor, which means to purify or to be made clean or pure by purifying one's self. This in no way approximates the "pureness" (from Heb. חה, taher, clean, pure, unadulterated) of the Words of God or the Son of God, who is without sin.

In addition, a person who is *"pure"* (ברר barar = purified, purged, make bright, or cleansed) will shew himself to be "pure" (ברר barar) to others who are "pure" (ברר barar), but will contend with those who are not (2 Sam. 22:27, Jude 1:3). In contrast, the Lord and His Words are clean or pure (i.e. not needing to be cleansed) from the beginning and without need of refining, washing, or purifying. They are perfect (Deut. 32:4, Psa. 19:7, Rom. 12:2, 1 Co. 13:10).

Pure Substances

Many substances found in Scripture are defined as "pure." For example, *"pure frankincense"* (Lev. 24:7) is from the Hebrew word זך (zak), which is derived from the word, זכך (zakak), meaning to be made clean. The "pure" blood of the grape (Deut. 32:14) is from the Hebrew word צמ (chemer), which indicates a juice that is not mixed with other substances. The *"pure oil"* (1 Kg. 5:11) is from the Hebrew word כתית (kathiyth), which means oil from beaten olives, without any additions or substitutions. Thus, the Hebrew words underlying the word translated "pure" in these examples do not indicate substances that were never dirty or contaminated, but rather, substances that were cleansed in the manufacturing process.

Pure Words

The Lord and His Words *"for ever...settled in heaven"* are clean from the foundation of the earth and without the need of refining. They were pure and usable when recorded by the prophets and Apostles throughout the various dispensations. The recording of those "pure" Words began with the prophet Moses during the dispensation of the Law.

One might ask why the Lord waited until Moses to inscripturate His Words. It is obvious that God had a plan. He is testing man in every possible way through seven dispensations (seven being the number signifying completeness). He tested man in a perfect environment and innocence, then in the period of conscience, followed by periods of human government and patriarchal rule. Man failed the test every time. Starting with the dispensation of the law, God gave man pure Words written in Hebrew. However, man failed again in spite of having written Words before him; just as he will fail in this dispensation, the church age, and the one to follow, the millennial age. The test is simple and some individuals have passed the test in every dispensation. God simply asks us to believe and trust Him by *"the voice of the **words** of the Lord,"* which *"are **pure** words"* made possible by His grace (Psa. 12:6, Prov. 30:5, Rom. 10:17,

Eph. 2:8-9). They are Words given by inspiration *"once"* (2 Tim. 3:15-16, Jude. 1:3).

The Words Chosen by Mortal Man in Translations

Words chosen by a translator, who is a *"mortal man,"* are not "pure," "infallible," "inerrant," or "inspired." Man's Words retain authority if they are AFTs of the original Words of God in Hebrew/Aramaic/Greek. Some translators are obviously providentially guided by God, but that does not make the words chosen by them inspired. The Words the translators selected are accurate and faithful to the meaning of the original Words *"for ever...settled in heaven,"* but they are not *"pure"* or *"given by inspiration"* (God-breathed) as are the *received* original language Words of the Bible.

> *"Shall mortal man be more just than God? shall a man be more pure than his maker?"* (Job 4:17). *"But the wisdom that is **from above** is first **pure**, then peaceable, gentle, and easy to be intreated, full of mercy and good fruits, without partiality, and without hypocrisy"* (James 3:17).

If we attribute purity and inspiration to the translated Words of God in any language, we are in reality claiming double inspiration, double purity, and double Apostolic and prophet-like men who chose them and who wrote them. It is equivalent to claiming that God gave His inspired Words twice, which is contrary to Scripture (Jude 1:3).

Furthermore, if we claim purity and inspiration for only one specific translation and translators, such as the King James Bible and its translators, we are again making similar "double" claims. One must quickly ask if other translations are inspired such as the Peshitta, Old

Latin, French Olivetan, the German Luther Bible, the Geneva Bible, he Tyndale Bible, the Great Bible, the Reina Valera Gomez, Smith-Van Dyke Bible in Arabic, Ostervold French Bible, Italian Diodati Bible, and many other translations. "*I trow* (think) *not!*" The translators were simply doing what God commanded (Lk. 17:9, Rom. 16:25-27, 1 Cor 14:21, Jer. 23:28-29) using His foundational Words which will be "*for ever*" established without change. We can reproduce God's Words faithfully through translating, but to claim the Words chosen by mere "*mortal man*" are "*given by inspiration*" and as "*pure*" as are God's Words is heretical. The translated words can be accurate and faithful, but inspired and pure goes a little too far for this author. The inspired, pure Words were given "*once*" (Jude. 1:3). Also:

> "*...as we were allowed of God to be put in trust with the gospel, even so **we speak; not as pleasing men, but God, which trieth our hearts**.*" (1 Thessalonians 2:4).

The Words of God Are As Pure As the Son

Our God, who did all of these things, is beyond description. There is no better attempt at describing Him than *The Westminster Confession of Faith*. It declares:

> "There is but one only living and true God, who is infinite in being and perfection, a most pure spirit, invisible, without body, parts, or passions, immutable, immense, eternal, incomprehensible, almighty, most wise, most holy, most free, most absolute, working all things according to the counsel of his own immutable and most righteous will, for his own glory; most loving, gracious, merciful, long-suffering, abundant in goodness and truth, forgiving iniquity, transgression, and sin; the rewarder of them that diligently seek him; and withal most just and terrible in his judgments, hating all sin, and who will by no means clear the guilty. God hath all life, glory, goodness, blessedness, in and of himself;

and is alone in and unto himself all-sufficient, not standing in need of any creatures which he hath made, nor deriving any glory from them, but only manifesting his own glory in, by, unto, and upon them: he is the alone fountain of all being, of whom, through whom, and to whom, are all things; and hath most sovereign dominion over them, to do by them, for them, and upon them, whatsoever himself pleaseth. In his sight all things are open and manifest; his knowledge is infinite, infallible, and independent upon the creature, so as nothing is to him contingent or uncertain. He is most holy in all his counsels, in all his works, and in all his commands. To him is due from angels and men, and every other creature, whatsoever worship, service, or obedience, he is pleased to require of them....

Chafer said the following about this description:

"It is probable that no more comprehensive declaration respecting God has been framed than this; yet it is precisely this infinity of Being which the Scriptures predicate of Christ." [41]

Job clearly attests to God's perfection:

"Canst thou by searching find out God? canst thou find out the Almighty unto perfection? It is as high as heaven; what canst thou do? deeper than hell; what canst thou know? The measure thereof is longer than the earth, and broader than the sea" (Job 11:7-9).

Other verses attest to our indescribable God and the Words that He speaks.

"Behold, God is great, and we know him not, neither can the number of his years be searched out" (Job 36:26).

---

[41] Lewis Sperry Chafer, *Systematic Theology* (Kregel Publications, Grand Rapids, MI, Vol. 5, 1993) 7-8.

"O LORD, how great are thy works! and thy thoughts are very deep" (Psalms 92:5, cf. 139:6, 145:3, 147:5, Rom. 33-34).

"Hear ye the word which the LORD speaketh unto you...the LORD is the true God, he is the living God, and an everlasting king: at his wrath the earth shall tremble, and the nations shall not be able to abide his indignation" (Jeremiah 10:10).

*"As for God, his way is **perfect: the word of the LORD is tried**: he is a buckler to all those that trust in him"* (Psalms 18:30).

Did God speak English, Spanish, Korean, Coptic, or other language words as the pure Words of God? Which Words were "tried" by God and given to man to record? Few true believers would deny the purity and perfection of God. However, this age, like the last age of the law, continues to be a sad testimony to Him and to His "pure" inscripturated Words because of the uncertainty created about His certain Words (Pro. 22:21). Many teachers have confused many students by making many false claims. Anything and everything is called "pure."

If believers accept the Trinity as described above and in the Scriptures, how can they deny the inspiration, certainty, perfection, and purity of the sure Words of God, which He calls *"my words?"* Or how can teachers or scholars deny any of the *"pure"* Words given *"once,"* simply because God chose to use gifted men to record His Words? Without a doubt, some AFTs by gifted men were providentially guided, but they are not inspired. Chafer said:

> "Few, indeed, will contend that any Person of the Godhead is not perfect, or that any word God speaks will not be as pure as He is pure. The element of doubt intrudes whenever and wherever the human element is combined with that which is divine."[42]

---

[42] Ibid. Vol. 6, 72 (Chafer).

It is well known to students of the Scriptures that the pure incarnate Word of God gave the pure inscripturated Words of Scripture. Subsequently, they are spiritually inseparable in significance and similarity.

> "The term Λογος (Logos-Word) is used in the New Testament about two hundred times to indicate God's Word written, and seven times to indicate the Son of God-the Living Word of God (John 1:1, 14; 1 John 1:1; 5:7; Rev 19:13); and it is important to recognize that in either of these forms of the Logos both the divine and human elements appear in supernatural union. These two forms of the Logos are subject to various comparisons: They are, alike, the *Truth* (John 14; 6; 17:17); *Everlasting* (Ps 119:89; Matt 24:34, 35; 1 Pet 1:25); *Life* (John 11:25; 14:6; 1 Pet 1:23; 1 John 1:1); *Saving* (Acts 16:31; 1 Cor 15:2); *Purifying* (Titus 2:14; 1 Pet 1:22); *Sanctifying* (John 17:17; Heb 10:14); *Beget Life* (1 Pet 1:23; Jas 1:18); *Judge* (John 6:26, 27; 12:48); *Glorified* (Romans 15:9; Acts 13:48). While *Theology* is the θεολογία (*theologia*, or ology of God), the Λογος of God is the expression of God-whether it be in Living or Written form."[43]

Our God gave us Words in Hebrew/Aramaic/Greek that are pure, preserved, inerrant, perfect, infallible, available, and *"received"* by *"all generations"* as the Words were progressively revealed. How any other words could be called *"pure,"* "unchangeable," *"perfect,"* and the *"foundation"* is beyond this author! Although many accusations have been made against the *received* original Words, no allegation has been able to hold up under the lens of His Words and careful evaluation of them by illumination. Dr. Chafer said:

> "Finally, much is made of alleged "contradictions," "inaccuracies," and "inconsistencies." It is pointed out with much assurance that an inerrant book could present no such

---

[43] Ibid. Vol. 4, 398 (Chafer).

problems. But who is the judge? If the Bible contains errors as seen by God, the case would be serious; if it contains errors as seen by men, the difficulty may be wholly accounted for in the sphere of human misunderstandings. The latter possibility is but little in evidence in the writings of the opposers of the Bible doctrine of inspiration. The Spirit of God has declared "Every word of God is pure" (Prov. 30:5); "The words of Jehovah are pure words: as silver tried in a furnace of earth, purified seven times" (Ps. 12:6); "The law of Jehovah is perfect, converting the soul" (Ps. 19:7); and, "As for God, his way is perfect; the word of Jehovah is tried" (Ps. 18:30). Confronted with such statements as these, a man of reason and candor will at least give some consideration to the possibility that the supposed errors in the Bible might seem to be such because of human limitations."[44]

Pure Righteousness

Man is not pure and man's words are not pure; any substance from earth is not pure, except the flesh of the God-man, Jesus Christ. Everything else on earth must be purified because of the fall of man. "*Pure*" righteousness comes only from God's covering of sinful man by His precious blood. "Pure" righteousness is imputed because of the work of our Saviour on the Cross. Chafer said:

"That there is a righteousness which the believer may possess wholly apart from any works or effort of his own and as a gift from God (cf. Rom. 5:17) is pure revelation and devoid of any confirmatory experience; besides, this bestowed righteousness is the only righteousness which God accepts in time or eternity. He Himself, being infinitely righteous, can receive nothing less than that which He is personally. Since present salvation is unto eternal and intimate association with God in His abode up in the highest glory, the necessity of being qualified for that sphere with a perfection which goes beyond human ability to provide is obvious. Thus the Apostle writes: "Giving thanks unto the

---

[44] Ibid. Vol. 1, 66 (Chafer).

Father, which hath made us meet to be partakers of the inheritance of the saints in light" (Col. 1:12). Respecting that righteousness which is God's gift through His Son,...in answer to [man's] faith." [45] [my addition, HDW]

Furthermore, the inspiration of the Scriptures declared in thousands of passages with Words such as *"thus saith the Lord," "God said,"* and *"it is written,"* cannot be separated from the purity of God's Words.

"Referring to the Epistle to the Hebrews, Olshausen writes: "In this remarkable epistle, God, or the Holy Ghost, is continually named as the speaker in the passages quoted from the Old Testament; and this not merely in those of which it is said in the context of the Old Testament Scriptures, 'God said,' but also in those in which some human being speaks, e. g. David, as composer of a Psalm. In this the view of the author clearly expresses itself as to the Old Testament and its writers. He regarded God as the Principle that lived, and wrought, and spoke in them all by his Holy Spirit; and accordingly Holy Scripture was to him **a pure work of God, although announced to the world by man**" (*Die Echtheit des N.T.*, p. 170, cited by Manly, *Bible Doctrine of Inspiration*, p. 172)."[46] "Similarly, seven attributes of the Bible are named in Psalm 119. These are: *faithful* (vs. 86), *broad* (vs. 96), *right* (vs. 128), *wonderful* (vs. 129), *pure* (vs. 140), *everlasting* (vs. 160), and *righteous* (vs. 172). The New Testament adds that the Word of God is *truth* (John 17:17), *profitable* (2 Tim. 3:16), *quick* and *powerful* (Heb. 4:12)."[47]

Many influential and godly men have held up their translation of the "pure" Words of God, the KJB, and called it the "standard" by which to measure other versions, but not a source to **correct** translations in

---

[45] Ibid. Vol. 6, 154 (Chafer).
[46] Ibid. Vol 1, 71-72 (Chafer).
[47] Ibid. Vol 1, 120 (Chafer).

other languages. It can be used as a guide, but the *"foundation"* is the original, preserved, pure Words of God. David Otis Fuller said:

> "I urge my listener to keep before him the KJV as the one safe, sure standard to go by in measuring other versions."[48]

The KJB is a safe "standard" in English. It has imputed authority. There is no equal to this English translation as a guide, but it should not be regarded as the pure inspired Words of God. We can hold up our English King James Bible and say it is the Word of God preserved in English. But to hold up **any** translation, including the KJB, and call it inspired or the "pure" Words of God, is improper, wrong, and possibly blasphemous.

This author cannot comprehend the difficulty in understanding these important principles.

> "All education proceeds on the principle that the learner has capacity to receive the instruction imparted. There must be a latent ability which needs only to be awakened by the challenge which the facts present. In the knowledge of God, children receive the truth more readily than adults. This is not a feature of *immaturity*. It is due to *purity*. "... the pure in heart: for they shall see God." [49]

Inaccurate teachings concerning these issues have encouraged many teachers and scholars in institutions of higher learning to ignore the original languages. In addition, the fear by many pastors that a person in the pew will not understand "pure," or be confused about what is an accurate and faithful translation is to belittle the man in the pew. God gave the church pastors who are to help men understand "the things of

---

[48] David Otis Fuller, quoted from http://av1611.com/kjbp/articles/fuller-preserved.html. Accessed 10/23/07.
[49] Chafer, op. cit., 132-133. (*Systematic Theology,* Vol. 1).

God." This governmental decision for the church was made in eternity past before the foundation of the world. God gifted men to be shepherds of His flock and to help believers understand God's methods. It is a crime to consider words given by man to be equivalent to the pure Words of a Holy God or not to make very apparent the **difference** between the *"pure"* or *"clean"* things versus things needing purification (Eze. 22:26). In the following quote, remember that holy is often translated "pure."

> "Beyond the offense which sin is to God's government, and beyond the injury it is to that which is the indisputable property of God, it, because of its immoral nature, outrages and insults the holy Person of God. **He is infinitely pure and righteous**. The prophet of old has said, "Thou art of **purer** eyes than to behold evil, and canst not look on iniquity: wherefore lookest thou upon them that deal treacherously, and holdest thy tongue when the wicked devoureth the man that is more righteous than he?" (Hab. 1:13), and the Apostle John has written: "This then is the message which we have heard of him, and declare unto you, that God is light, and in him is no darkness at all" (1 John 1:5). So, also, the Apostle James declares: "Let no man say when he is tempted, I am tempted of God: for God cannot be tempted with evil, neither tempteth he any man" (James 1:13). When the truth is considered apart from all relationships, there is no argument respecting the **holiness** of God; yet this is the very truth which measures the sinfulness of sin. It is the fact that God is transparently **holy** which lends meaning to such terms as *ungodliness, defilement*, and *impiety*. [50]

We must be careful what we call holy, pure, clean, or without need of cleansing.

The men chosen to record the "pure" Words of God were sinners, who were not inspired. Even so, they were used of God to receive the Words of faith *"once delivered"* (Jude 1:3). Why is this so hard to

---

[50] Chafer, op. cit., 257-258 (*Systematic Theology,* Vol. 2).

understand? Why are men from America traveling all over the world declaring the KJB is inspired and pure? Some are even declaring that people all over the world must learn English in order to read the Word of God.[51] They are insulting people in other nations because of their arrogance, pride, and lack of humbleness toward men in other language-groups. Men in other countries who speak languages other than English are great students of God's Words and excellent translators of His Words into the languages of the world. The pride and lack of humility by so many good saints who carelessly use the words pure and inspiration is overt sin that is rarely recognized by many. They seem to have a blind spot.

The Scriptures bear an uncomplicated testimony to the sinfulness of man; even the sins of those who wrote the Bible are exposed. The Old Testament declares: "For there is no man that sinneth not" (1 Kings 8:46); "For in thy sight shall no man living be justified" (Ps. 143:2); "Who can say, I have made my heart clean, I am **pure** from my sin?" (Prov. 20:9); "For there is not a just man on the earth, that doeth good, and sinneth not" (Eccl. 7:20). With the same end in view, the New Testament is even more emphatic. The universal practice of sin is presupposed by Christ (cf. Matt. 4:17; Mark 1:15; 6:12; Luke 24:47; John 3:3–5). The preaching of the gospel is itself an implication that salvation is needed by all. Apart from redemption, man is wrong in the sight of God. Those who fail to receive the saving grace of God are in every instance condemned. The very universality of Christ's death indicates the truth that God sees a lost world of men for whom He gave His Son (2 Cor. 5:14–15). Many direct statements appear in the New Testament. A few only need be quoted: "What then? are we better than they? No, in no wise: for we have before proved both Jews and Gentiles, that they are all under sin" (Rom. 3:9); "Now we know that what things soever the law saith, it saith to them who are under the law: that every mouth may be stopped,

---

[51] This kind of statement occurred on a television program anchored by John Ankerberg when several men participated in a discussion about the 'new' versions and the King James Bible.

and all the world may become guilty before God. Therefore by the deeds of the law there shall no flesh be justified in his sight: for by the law is the knowledge of sin" (Rom. 3:19–20); "For all have sinned, and come short of the glory of God" (Rom. 3:23); "But the scripture hath concluded all under sin, that the promise by faith of Jesus Christ might be given to them that believe" (Gal. 3:22); "If we say that we have not sinned, we make him a liar, and his word is not in us" (1 John 1:10).[52]

Many men are defending **their** position, that the English-speaking people have a "pure" Bible and no one else in the world does. Have they stopped to talk with men in other nations? This author has and the comments have been very negative toward men from America who are making such claims. They are astonished at the claims. Those claiming a select translation as pure and/or inspired probably don't even realize what they have done.

> "*Woe unto them that call evil good, and good evil; that put darkness for light, and light for darkness; that put bitter for sweet, and sweet for bitter!*" (Isaiah 5:20).

Even Mormons recognize the folly of the superficial claims of misguided men. It has encouraged them to be more aggressive and to make claims of their own. For example, one Mormon website said:

"Trying to challenge my beliefs, I've had a few people tell me the Bible is the only word of God. *Is it?* Where has God ever said the Bible is his only words to us today? Which translation of the Bible? King James? New International Version? New Revised Standard Version? Revised English Bible? Each of the many versions of the Bible renders verses a little differently, giving a slightly different meaning to them. It is impossible to translate anything word for word with exactly the same meaning from

---

[52] Chafer, op. cit. 281-282 (*Systematic Theology*, Vol. 2).

one language to another which is one of the reasons of the differences. The bible states that the truth of all things will be established by two or more witness. The Book of Mormon is God's second book of scripture to witness to us the divinity of Jesus Christ and his teachings of the Gospel. To disqualify The Book of Mormon as scripture people always quote Revelation 22:18:-19 to me."[53]

Some of these issues arose at a recent meeting concerning the use of the word "pure" related to the Scriptures and the sometimes mystical, arrogant American attitude.

Significant Questions and Answers at a Dean Burgon Society Conference

The following discussion occurred at a Dean Burgon Society meeting in Chicago, IL, at Ravenswood Baptist Church concerning preservation and the "pure" Words of God. A person in the audience asked:

"When we talk about preservation in terms of the King James Bible, "Are we without error?"

This author answered:

"We have not found any errors. However, in translation there may be words that perhaps might be better, but it is not an error."

For example, spelling changes in words used in the King James Bible editions have been noted, as well as archaic words. Furthermore,

---

[53] They use Pro. 30:6-7 on the website as justification. (http://salvation.scottsworld.info/bible.htm)

there may be several words with the same meaning, but the King James translators chose one. Were they in error to have used the words they chose instead of another? Of course not. Is it an error to change a word in a translation because of spelling changes? Of course not. The person in the audience continued by stating:

> "Does it not cease to be pure then? Don't we cease to be pure if I put my finger in my mouth; doesn't it cease to be pure water if we have something different; pure words the Bible tells us."

This person answered his own question. The saliva in his mouth was not "pure" to begin with, and putting his finger in his mouth would change it very little. The human mouth is a very filthy place; more filthy than the mouth of a dog. This is a very important principle in Scripture. Anything defiled, unclean, or impure that touches something undefiled, clean, or pure, causes it to become impure in every way (Hag. 2:12-14). Furthermore, the original Words of God are pure and perfect as to spelling and word order and meaning. Any change in God's original inspired Words would render them unsuitable as **a foundation**, which would include **any** change in spelling, word order, addition, or subtraction. However, changing a word in a translation (i.e. spelling changes) cannot be compared to changing the original *received* Words. Spelling or necessary syntactic word changes would not destroy a translation that is accurate and faithful. This author continued by stating:

> "Well, when we start trying to define "*pure*"—do you use "*pure*" in terms of the inspired Words or in terms of the English words that were chosen? It is a matter of definition."

In other words, do you consider your definition of "pure" **the same** when applied to God and His Words as when applied to a translation? "*I trow not.*" Dr. Waite added:

> "I just want to amplify that. I read from page 3 of our [Dean Burgon Society] articles of faith, 'We believe the King James Version, the Authorized Version of the English Bible, is a true, faithful, and accurate translation. We use these three words, we stand on it; of these two providentially preserved texts, that is the Masoretic text and Greek Received Text, which in our time has no equal among of all the other English translations. The translators did such a fine job in their translation that we can hold up our Authorized Version of King James and say this is the word of God without apology.' So we don't say pure, we don't say inspired, we don't say inerrant, we don't say infallible…We don't say [the King James Bible] is errant, fallible; we don't say impure.
>
> We prefer not to use those strong words for God Himself. As for God, His way is perfect. He is pure. He is holy. He is infallible. His Hebrew and Greek Words are infallible. They are God-breathed. They are inerrant. They are pure. They are perfect. There is nothing that matches them. There is nothing that man does that can be classified this way. So, we diminish some of these terms that are used by others. We don't want to be overly hyperbolic and not over the top; it is a dangerous situation.

Dr. Mike Monte, Pastor of Robbinsdale Baptist Church in Minnesota, added:

> "Some of the confusion on that comes from the fact that people characteristically want to become mystical about a translation. I think that's what sometimes occurs and we understand that God inspired the original autographs; [He] gave them by the prophets by inspiration; that as those have been translated, someone may chose one word over another as they are doing with the Spanish Bible and there is also all sorts of criteria in the selecting of individual words as far as that goes. But we are looking at the process of inspiration as

having occurred with the autographs and if we remove it from the autographs, we have bought for ourselves a world of hurt. Then we have pilgrim fathers of course rejected the KJB and held to the versions which they were used to because they did not like the KJB, we have historical problems, we have problems with other cultures as we do with the Spanish because the Mexicans think it's the gringos messing around with their Bible and that we think we're superior in everything and it runs into problems. We have to stick to what God has inspired and then work with translations."

Dr. Waite added the following words to this recorded discussion:

"I just want to say that I have not found any translation errors in the KJB, in other words the Hebrew or Aramaic or Greek Words may have four or five different accurate meanings—the King James Bible translators pick one of the five and apply it, others could be picked, it would still be right, but they picked this one.

Secondly, they used at least one grammatical, contextual rule of Hebrew or Greek grammar. Other points could be used but they chose at least one. When people point out the [alleged] error of the King James Bible when going over: 'teach all nations, baptizing, etc.,' they say, "Teach? Teach is not the imperative!" And they criticize the King James translators...What they didn't know is the participle in the Greek language can also be used as an imperative. And the King James translators, astute as they were in the Hebrew and Greek language, knew that and they used it and our Greek "gringos" did not know this."

Why should not everyone, who has fallen into the trap of claiming a translation is pure and inspired, repent and be washed with *"pure water," "delivered once,"* which declares the inspired Words of God are *"pure?"*

*"Let us draw near with a true heart in full assurance of faith, having our hearts sprinkled from an evil conscience, and our bodies washed with **pure water**"*

(Hebrews 10:22). *"Seeing **ye have purified** your souls **in obeying the truth through the Spirit** unto unfeigned love of the brethren, see that ye love one another with a **pure** heart fervently"* (1 Peter 1:22).

God's Words Have Been Preserved For Ever

Were God's Words given in English at the first? Of course not![54] Revelation of the Words of God, which were inscripturated by His prophets and Apostles, were given in Hebrew, Aramaic, and Greek. It is those Words, which serve as the "foundation" for all translations and which are necessary for obedience to our Lord's command: *"Teaching them to observe all things whatsoever I have commanded you"* (Mat. 28:20). Well-trained pastors in any language-group will consult the original Words *received* in the Hebrew Masoretic Text and the Greek Traditional/Received Text when necessary, which are preserved *"for ever."*

> (1 Peter 1:23) *"Being born again, not of corruptible seed, but of incorruptible, by the word of God which **liveth and abideth forever**."*
> (Psa. 12:6-7) *"The words of the Lord are pure words: as silver tried in a furnace of earth, purified seven times. Thou shalt keep them, O Lord, thou shalt preserve them **from this generation forever**."*
> (Psa. 111:7-8) *"The works of his hands are verity and judgment; all his commandments are sure. **They stand fast for ever and ever**, and are done in truth and uprightness."*
> (Isa. 40:8) *"The grass withereth, the flower fadeth: but the word of our God **shall stand for ever**."*

---

[54] This author is aware of G. A. Riplinger's belief that English translations were early and inspired, which is her privilege. She is a good sister in Christ. However, we must ask, "Was the Peshitta, Aramaic, Latin, etc., which were early, also inspired?" *"I trow not!"*

(Psa. 117:2) "... *the truth of the Lord endureth for ever. Praise ye the Lord.*"
(Psa. 119:152) "*Concerning thy testimonies, I have known of old that* ***thou hast founded them for ever.***"
(Psa. 119:160) "*Thy word is true from the beginning: and every one of thy righteous judgments* **endureth for ever.**"

Why not declare the Words pure that were preserved for every generation? Why not declare the translations based upon the received Masoretic Hebrew and Traditional/Received Greek texts into many language-groups by the use of verbal and formal equivalent translating techniques accurate and faithful (AFTs)? Why should English-speaking people continue to insult others around the world by declaring that we have the Words of God? Why not humble ourselves? To whom shall they go? The Lord *"hast the words of eternal life."* Why not support the aims and goals of groups like "Bearing Precious Seed International"[55] that encourage saints around the world to translate God's original language Words into their language?

Perhaps it is time for believing men everywhere to anticipate their death and the judgment seat of Christ. Perhaps it is time for men everywhere to request the inscription that the famous astronomer, Copernicus, requested to be engraved on his final resting place:

> "I crave not for the favor which Paul received, nor the grace with which thou didst pardon Peter, but only that mercy which thou didst bestow upon the penitent thief on the cross."[56]

It is time for men everywhere to recognize that the pure Words of God are available for all people, kindred, tongues, and nations, without respect of persons. They are available to those who are seeking them. We

---

[55] Dr. Steve Zeinner, Director, www.bpsglobal.org.
[56] J. Aall Ottesen Stub, *Verbal Inspiration* (Lutheran Publishing House, Decorah, Iowa, 1915) 106.

must help make them immediately available. Any claim to the contrary shows disrespect for the Lord Himself. The original Words are available to be translated. The Lord said:

> *"In the law it is written, With men of other tongues and other lips will I speak unto this people"* (1 Corinthians 14:21).

and

> *"If a man love me, he will keep my words"* (Jn. 14:23)

AMEN!

HEBREW, ARAMAIC, GREEK, & ENGLISH WORDS RELATED TO PURE IN THE KING JAMES BIBLE

Hebrew Greek English Word	Strongs/Webster Definition	Verse Examples
Pure:	PURE, a. *L. purus.* **1.** Separate from all heterogeneous or extraneous matter; clear; free from mixture; as pure water; pure clay; pure sand; pure air; pure silver or gold. Pure wine is very scare. **2.** Free from moral defilement; without spot; not sullied or tarnished; incorrupt; undebased by moral turpitude; holy. *"Thou art of purer eyes than to behold evil."* (Hab.1. Prov.20.) **3.** Genuine; real; true; incorrupt; unadulterated; as pure religion. James 1. **4.** Unmixed; separate from any other subject or from every thing foreign; as pure mathematics. **5.** Free from guilt; guiltless; innocent. "No hand of strife is pure, but that which wins." **6.** Not vitiated with improper or corrupt words or phrases; as a pure style of discourse or composition. **7.** Disinterested; as	

	pure benevolence. **8.** Chaste; as a pure virgin. **9.** Free from vice or moral turpitude. Tit.1. **10.** Ceremonially clean; unpolluted. Ezra 6. **11.** Free from any thing improper; as, his motives are pure. **12.** Mere; absolute; that and that only; unconnected with any thing else; as a pure villain. He did that from pure compassion, or pure good nature. PURE, v.t. To purify; to cleanse. *Not in use.*	
Hebrew Greek English Word	Strongs/Webster Definition	Verse Examples
Heb. 2889 חהור tahowr	pure (in a physical, chemical, ceremonial or moral sense):--clean, fair, pure(-ness).	"The thoughts of the wicked *are* an abomination to the LORD: but *the words* of the **pure** *are* pleasant words." (Proverbs 15:26, cf. Psa. 19:9, Pro. 30:12, Hab. 1:13) [Occurs eighty-seven times, translated equally pure or clean, once fair, primary meaning is pureness; e.g. already pure without needing to cleaned or purified, a clean animal that has no defects—does not need repairing. HDW]
Heb. 2134 זכ zak	clear:--clean, pure.	"And thou shalt command the children of Israel, that they bring thee **pure** oil olive beaten for the light, to cause the lamp to burn always." (Exodus 27:20) [Occurs in eleven verses, translated clean twice, HDW]
Heb. 1865	from an unused root (meaning to move	"Take thou also unto thee principal spices, of **pure** myrrh five hundred *shekels,* and of sweet cinnamon half

דְּרוֹר *derore'*	rapidly); freedom; hence, spontaneity of outflow, and so clear:--liberty, pure.	so much, *even* two hundred and fifty *shekels*, and of sweet calamus two hundred and fifty *shekels*," (Exodus 30:23) [This word occurs seven times and is translated liberty six times, HDW]
Heb. 2561 צֶמֶר chemer	from 2560; wine (as fermenting):--X pure, red wine. See Hebrew 2560	"Butter of kine, and milk of sheep, with fat of lambs, and rams of the breed of Bashan, and goats, with the fat of kidneys of wheat; and thou didst drink the **pure** blood of the grape." (Deuteronomy 32:14) Occurs only twice, translated red wine or pure blood, HDW] see Isa. 27:2
Heb. 1305 בָּרַר barar	a primitive root; to clarify (i.e. brighten), examine, select:--make bright, choice, chosen, cleanse (be clean), clearly, polished, (shew self) pure(-ify), purge (out).	"With the **pure** thou wilt shew thyself [the Lord] pure; and with the froward thou [the Lord] wilt shew thyself unsavoury." (2 Samuel 22:27) [Occurs in sixteen verses; primary meaning is to purge out or to shew cleanness, pureness, HDW]
Heb. 3795 כָּתִית kathiyth	from 3807; beaten, i.e. pure (oil): -beaten. See Hebrew 3807	"And Solomon gave Hiram twenty thousand measures of wheat *for* food to his household, and twenty measures of **pure** oil: thus gave Solomon to Hiram year by year." (1 Kings 5:11) [Occurs five times, four times beaten, once pure, HDW]
Heb. 5462 וּגַּר cagar	a primitive root; to shut up; figuratively, to surrender:--close up, deliver (up), give over (up), inclose, X pure, repair, shut (in, self, out, up, up together), stop, X straitly.	"So Solomon overlaid the house within with **pure** gold: and he made a partition by the chains of gold before the oracle; and he overlaid it with gold." 1 Kings 6:21 [Occurs eighty-seven times; primary meaning close or shut up; HDW]
Heb. 2141 זָכַךְ zakak	a primitive root (compare 2135); to be transparent or clean (phys. or morally):--be (make) clean, be pure(-r).	"Her Nazarites were **purer** than snow, they were whiter than milk, they were more ruddy in body than rubies, their polishing *was* of sapphire:" (Lamentations 4:7) [Occurs four times; primarily

	See Hebrew 2135	cleaned, HDW]
Heb. 1249 בַּר bar *bar*	from 1305 (in its various senses); beloved; also pure, empty:--choice, clean, clear, pure. See Hebrew 1305	"The statutes of the LORD *are* right, rejoicing the heart: the commandment of the LORD *is* **pure**, enlightening the eyes." (Psalms 19:8) [Used seven times, used as clear, clean, or pure, not purified, HDW]
Heb. 6337 פָּז paz	from 6338; pure (gold); hence, gold itself (as refined):--fine (pure) gold. See Hebrew 6338	"I will make a man more precious than **fine** gold; even a man than the golden wedge of Ophir." (Isaiah 13:12) "For thou preventest him with the blessings of goodness: thou settest a crown of **pure** gold on his head." (Psalms 21:3) [Occurs nine times, primarily pure gold, HDW]
Heb. 6884 צָרַף tsaraph	a primitive root; to fuse (metal), i.e. refine (literally or figuratively):--cast, (re-)fine(-er), founder, goldsmith, melt, pure, purge away, try.	"Thy word *is* very **pure**: therefore thy servant loveth it." (Psalms 119:140) [Occurs twenty-nine times; used primarily as refine[r] or tried, HDW]
Heb. 2891 חָהַר taher	a primitive root; properly, to be bright; i.e. (by implication) to be pure (physical sound, clear, unadulterated; Levitically, uncontaminated; morally, innocent or holy):--be (make, make self, pronounce) clean, cleanse (self), purge, purify(-ier, self).	"And he shall sit *as* a refiner [tsaraph 6884] and **purifier** of silver: and he shall **purify** the sons of Levi, and purge them as gold and silver, that they may offer unto the LORD an offering in righteousness." (Mal. 3:3, cf. Eze. 39:14) [Occurs seventy-nine times, primarily as purifying or made clean]
Heb. 5343 (Aramaic) נְקֵא nekay'	(Aramaic) from a root corresponding to 5352; clean:--pure. See Hebrew 5352	"I beheld till the thrones were cast down, and the Ancient of days did sit, whose garment *was* white as snow, and the hair of his head like the **pure** wool: his throne *was like* the fiery flame, *and* his wheels *as* burning fire." (Daniel 7:9) [The only occurrence, HDW]
Heb.	a primitive root	"What *is* man, that he should be

2135 זכה zakah	(compare 2141); to be translucent; figuratively, to be innocent:--be (make) clean, cleanse, be clear, count pure. See Hebrew 2141	**clean**? and *he which is* born of a woman, that he should be righteous?" (Job 15:14) "Shall I count *them* **pure** with the wicked balances, and with the bag of deceitful weights?" (Micah 6:11) [Occurs in eight verses, used primarily as innocent, HDW]
Gr. 2513 κατηαρος kath-ar-os'	of uncertain affinity; clean (literally or figuratively):--clean, clear, pure.	"Now ye are **clean** through the word which I have spoken unto you." (John 15:3) "Holding the mystery of the faith in a **pure** conscience." (1 Timothy 3:9) [Occurs 24 times, used as pure—secondary to the indwelling and washing of the Word, HDW]
Gr. 53 ἁγίος hagnos'	from the same as 40; properly, clean, i.e. (figuratively) innocent, modest, perfect:--chaste, clean, pure. See Greek 40	"Lay hands suddenly on no man, neither be partaker of other men's sins: keep thyself **pure**." (1 Timothy 5:22) "And every man that hath this hope in him purifieth himself, even as he is **pure**." (1 John 3:3) [Occurs eight times, used primarily as separated unto God]
Gr. 1506 Ειλικρινης	from heile (the sun's ray) and 2919; judged by sunlight, i.e. tested as genuine (figuratively):--pure, sincere. See Greek 2919	"That ye may approve things that are excellent; that ye may be **sincere** and without offence till the day of Christ;" (Philippians 1:10) "This second epistle, beloved, I now write unto you; in *both* which I stir up your **pure** minds by way of remembrance:" (2 Peter 3:1) [Occurs only twice, HDW]

CHAPTER 2

RECEIVING AND KEEPING THE WORDS OF GOD

A COMMAND TO GOD'S PEOPLE "RECEIVE MY INSTRUCTION"

"**Receive my instruction,** and not silver; and knowledge rather than choice gold" (Proverbs 8:10). "Moreover he said unto me, Son of man, all **my words** that I shall speak unto thee receive in thine heart, and hear with thine ears" (Ezekiel 3:10) "For this cause also thank we God without ceasing, because, when ye **received** the word of God which ye heard of us, ye **received** it not as the word of men, but as it is in truth, the word of God, which effectually worketh also in you that believe" (1 Thessalonians 2:13).

"IF A MAN LOVE ME, HE WILL KEEP MY WORDS"

"Jesus answered and said unto him, If a man love me, he will **keep** my words: and my Father will love him, and we will come unto him, and make our abode with him" (John 14:23).

Introduction

You may have been misinformed concerning the meaning or interpretation of the underlined phrases in the verses above and in many similar verses. The purpose of this chapter is to correct misunderstanding and misapplications concerning the intent, purpose, and application of "*receive*" and "*keep*" in many verses of Scripture.

The Problems

Three significant problems are identified. First, one of the most significant problems observed in these last days is the propensity of God's people to question God's Words because of the prevailing atmosphere of *uncertainty* in the postmodern age. This grievous *uncertainty* concerning **Truth** follows on the heels of the recent tendency of God's assemblies to neither *receive* nor *keep* the exact precise inspired Words given by revelation and inscripturated. The Words were received and recorded by God's Apostles and prophets as instructed in His inspired, inerrant, infallible, preserved, pure Words (e.g., Ex. 34:1, Prov. 8:10, 10:8, Isa. 30:8, Jer. 32:33, Eze. 3:10, 1 Thess. 2:13, Jn. 17:8).

Secondly, it appears the act of *receiving* His Words is undermined by the constant attack on their **preservation.** In addition, the **method of their preservation** is poorly understood. The God-ordained method will be discussed briefly below.

The third problem, which is related to the first two, is the dereliction of duty in *keeping* the Words of God by so many people who profess the name of Jesus Christ in His church (Jn. 14:15, 21-23). This is a very serious disregard of a critical duty commanded by our Lord. *Keeping* His Words does not mean just to "*obey*" or "*do*," as many people think, but it also means to preserve, guard, watch over, and protect His Words from corruption (see below). To God's glory, some have heeded and understood the commandment to "keep" His Words.

Serious Accusations

These are serious accusations, but they are not without foundation. They are confirmed in the writings of many authors and by witnessing the actions of many individuals through the centuries, particularly in this present age. The failure to understand clear Scriptural precepts[57] results from the inability to identify critical doctrinal verses in Scripture, from poor exegesis and teaching, and from the promotion of the Words of God as simply a message, which is not dependent upon precise, preserved Words to the *"jot and tittle."* The example of Israel's folly in old times should be enough to *"turn"* individuals, churches, institutions of higher learning, and nations to God and His Words (Psa. 80:3, Prov. 1:23, 1 Cor. 10:6, Rom. 15:4). However, people in all nations continue to *turn* their back on the Almighty and refuse to *receive, hear,* and *keep* His Words. They have rejected His instruction. They are unable to discern His Wisdom. They have turned to their own philosophies, which are constructed out of false and ungodly premises (Isa. 55:7-9).

> *"Hear, O earth: behold, I will bring evil upon this people, even the fruit of their thoughts, because they have not hearkened unto **my words**, nor to my law, but **rejected** it" (Jeremiah 6:19). "And they have **turned unto me the back**, and not the face: though I taught them, rising up early and teaching them, yet they have not hearkened to **receive** instruction" (Jeremiah 32:33).*

This is the tenor of many books released over the last several years, which exalt a preserved message, but not the exact preservation of

---

[57] Postmodernists call the absolute precepts, statutes, laws, and commandments in Scripture "propositions," as if they are proposals which can be refused, that is, they refuse to accept absolute Words that contain absolute directions—everything is up for discussion or rather deconstruction designed to eliminate authority.

the inerrant, infallible Words of God made available to every generation as promised in Scripture (e.g. Psa. 12:6-7, Psa. 100:5, 102:12, Psa. 117, 119:152, 160, Mat. 4:4, 5:17-18, 24:35, and many other places). These books include: *From the Mind of God to the Mind of Man* by James B. Williams, General Editor, and Randolf Shaylor, Managing Editor, (Ambassador-Emerald International, Greenville, SC, 4th printing, 2002) and also their book, *God's Word in Our Hands, The Bible Preserved For Us* (Ambassador-Emerald International, Greenville, SC, 2003); *God's Word Preserved* by Dr. Michael D. Sproul, (Whetstone Precepts Press, Tempe, AR, 2005); and *King James Onlyism: A New Sect* by James D. Price, (Saik Wah Press, PTE, LTD, Singapore, 2006).

The Scripture repeatedly charges us to "RECEIVE" the Words of God (used interchangeably with Word of God); and it charges us to **personally** "KEEP" (preserve) them. This author is convinced that it is the neglect of these personal acts, the act of *"receiving"* and the act of *"keeping"* His Word**s**, which is causing many of the problems with *"uncertainty"* that plague our churches today. The *"uncertainty"* extends to proper doctrine and application of doctrine along with a long list of other difficulties that arise as a result of not *receiving* His Words. This work is an attempt to encourage those who have gone astray, because of poor exegesis and teaching of God's Words, to perceive the error of not *receiving* and of not *keeping* God's Words. Scripture repeatedly indicates to *"receive and keep"* the Words of God.

Receiving His Words

In the upper room, our Lord prayed to the Father as the Apostles listened. He knew that the Apostles had *received* His Words and expressed it to the Father, saying:

*"For I have given unto them the words which thou gavest me; and they have **received** them, and have known surely that I came out from thee, and they have believed that thou didst send me"* (John 17:8).

Received in this verse comes from the Greek word, λαμβανω (lambanō). It carries the associated meanings of "to take hold," "be amazed," "catch," "have," and "take away" either figuratively or literally. It is more aggressive than many other words translated *"receive."*[58] It is the Greek word behind *"received"* in Romans 1:5. In this verse, Paul was relating that the Apostles had aggressively taken hold of the concept of grace with amazement to be promoted in all nations through the gospel *"for his name,"* the name above all names, the Word of God, who is the Lord Jesus Christ. The word lambano is in contrast to δεχομια (dechomia), which also is translated *"receive."* Dechomai has a more passive meaning (cf. Mat. 11:14, Jn. 4:45, Acts 3:21). For example, in John 4:45 the Galileans received the Lord Jesus Christ passively because of the miracles He had performed in Galilee and Jerusalem. They did not *"receive"* (lambano) Him in a way that would lead to salvation, but they *"received"* (dechomia) Him in a way that would **not** lead to salvation.

Receiving the Words of God Is an Act of Faith

In John 17:8 quoted above, please note that *receiving* is linked to believing in the Lord Jesus Christ, who was sent by the Father. Receiving is an act of faith; a faith that is sure. *"But without faith it is impossible to please him: for he that cometh to God must believe that he is, and that he is a rewarder of them that diligently seek him"* (Hebrews 11:6). The need to aggressively *receive* (lambano) His Words is constantly reinforced and

---

[58] Such as Strong's 5562, choreo; 618, apolambano; 308, anablepo; 3858, paradecomai; 588, apodecomai; 4355, proslambano;

repeated in Scripture. He gave them, but we must actively *receive* them (1 Thess. 2:13). As assuredly as the gift of salvation is free, His Words are a gift, freely given to anyone who will *receive* them. They are to be *received* as the *inspired* Words of God, which He promised to preserve **"to all generations"** (2 Tim. 3:15-16, Psa. 100:5, 111:7-8, 117:2, 119:152, 160, Isa. 40:8, etc., etc., etc.).

> *"The counsel of the LORD standeth for ever, the thoughts of his heart* **to all generations***"* (Psalms 33:11). *"For the LORD is good; his mercy is everlasting; and his truth endureth* **to all generations.***"* (Psalms 100:5)

The Apostle Peter affirmed this important doctrine, saying:

> *"Being born again, not of corruptible seed, but of incorruptible, by the word of God, which liveth and abideth* **for ever**. *For all flesh is as grass, and all the glory of man as the flower of grass. The grass withereth, and the flower thereof falleth away: But the word of the Lord* **endureth for ever**. *And this is the word which by the gospel is preached unto you"* (1 Peter 1:23-25).

Many are Victims of Scholars

The problem today is that many have fallen victim to the unrelenting proclamations of 'scholars,' who were not given the responsibility to preserve the Words, who claim that His Words are not all preserved, or who assert that they are not all readily available *"to all generations"* (Psa. 100:5). They make claims such as the Words are in "all the manuscripts," but not accessible to everyone, particularly a believer who is not a "textual critic." For example, Dr. James B. Williams and Dr. Randolph Shaylor claim:

"We believe that the Bible teaches that God providentially preserved His written Word (note that they do not say Words, HDW). This preservation exists in the **totality** of the ancient language manuscripts of that revelation. We are therefore certain that we possess the very Word of God."[59] (my addition, HDW).

They imply that Words could be hidden in secret places and possibly not available to anyone. This is contrary to clear Scriptural proclamations (see below). Furthermore, their statement would include well-known corrupted manuscripts such as Aleph (Sinaiticus), B (Vaticanus), A (Alexandrinus), Beza, and others. Their claim that "We are therefore certain that we possess the very Word of God" is mute and empty. How do they know we possess the very Word of God, if those words are in "the totality of the ancient language manuscripts" and if we do **not** have the original autographs? The only way to know and *receive* them is to believe God's Words, which proclaim His Truth that states they are available to every generation (see above). God says:

> *"I have not spoken in secret, in a dark place of the earth: I said not unto the seed of Jacob, Seek ye me in vain: I the LORD speak righteousness, I declare things that are right"* (Isaiah 45:19). *"Come ye near unto me, hear ye this; I have not spoken in secret from the beginning; from the time that it was, there am I: and now the Lord GOD, and his Spirit, hath sent me"* (Isaiah 48:16). *"For this commandment which I command thee this day, it is not hidden from thee, neither is it far off. It is not in heaven, that thou shouldest say, Who shall go up for us to heaven, and bring it unto us, that we may hear it, and do it? Neither is it beyond the sea, that thou shouldest say, Who shall go over the sea for us, and bring it unto us, that we may hear it, and do it? But the word is very nigh unto*

---

[59] James Williams, General Editor, and Randolph Shaylor, Managing Editor. *God's Word in Our Hands, The Bible Preserved For Us* (Ambassador Emerald International, Greenville, SC, 2003) iii.

***thee**, in thy mouth, and in thy heart, that thou mayest do it"* (Deuteronomy 30:11-14).

Tertullian (c.155–230) refuted these types of false claims very early in the apostolic age, saying:

> "I hold sure title-deeds from the **original** owners themselves...I am the heir of the Apostles just as they carefully prepared their **will** and **testament**, and committed it to a **trust**...**even so I hold it**."[60]

And he said:

> "run to the apostolic churches, in which the very thrones of the apostles are still pre-eminent in their places, IN WHICH THEIR OWN AUTHENTIC WRITINGS ARE READ, UTTERING THE VOICE AND REPRESENTING THE FACE OF EACH OF THEM SEVERALLY. Achaia is very near you, (in which) you find CORINTH. Since you are not far from Macedonia, you have PHILIPPI; (and there too) you have the THESSALONIANS. Since you are able to cross to Asia, you get EPHESUS. Since, moreover, you are close upon Italy, you have Rome, from which there comes even into our own hands the very authority (of the apostles themselves)" (Tertullian, *Prescription Against Heretics*).[61]

There are many other ante-Nicene church elders who affirmed their knowledge of the preservation and the method of preserving His Words, which is confirmed in the Scriptures (cf. Rom. 3:1-2, 1 Tim. 3:15). Clement of Rome (97-140 A. D.) said:

[60] H. D. Williams, M.D., Ph.D., *The Lie That Changed the Modern World, A Refutation of the Modernist's Cry: Poly-Scripturae* (Bible For Today Press, Collingswood, NJ, 2004) 116. This is a quote from Wilbur Pickering's book, *The Identity of the New Testament Church,* p. 108.
[61] David W. Cloud, *Faith vs. the Modern Bible Versions* (Way of Life Literature, Port Huron, MI, 2005) 74.

"Thus the humility and godly submission of so great and illustrious men have rendered not only us, but also **all the generations** before us, better; even as many as have **received** His oracles in fear and truth."[62] (my emphasis, HDW)

Dean John William Burgon repeatedly affirmed the preservation of His Words. The Words *received* have been preserved by the ingenious method designed by the Author:

"…it will be perceived that a three-fold security has been provided for the integrity of the Deposit:—Copies,— Versions,—Fathers."[63]

The Narrow Route Versus The Broad Route

The route God chose to preserve His Words that were to be *received* differs significantly from the route Satan chose. Satan's route had very little respect for the admonitions found in Deuteronomy 4:2, Proverbs 30:5-6, and Revelation 22:18-19. God's route is very narrow, whereas the route of the world is wide with great worldly influence (Mat. 7:13-16). The evidence provided by the narrow route, which preserved the Words of God through sanctified churches, is abundant. Dean John William Burgon and Edward Miller, Burgon's assistant, clearly attest to the evidence. Edward Miller wrote in the introduction to Dean John William Burgon (1813-1888), the Dean of Chichester's book, *The Causes of Corruption of the Traditional Text:*

---

[62] Clement of Rome, "The Epistle to the Corinthians" (*The Master Christian Library*, Ages Software, Version 8, Rio, WI, 2000) Chapter 19, p. 26.
[63] Dean John William Burgon, *The Traditional Text of the Holy Gospels* (Dean Burgon Society Press, Collingswood, NJ, Originally published 1896, republished 1998 by the DBS) 23.

> **"The Traditional Text,...has been traced back to the earliest ages** in the existence of those sacred writings...It is evident that the turning-point of the controversy between ourselves and the Neologian[64] school must lie in the centuries before St. Chrysostom. If, as Dr. Hort maintains, the Traditional Text not only gained supremacy at that era but did not exist in the early ages, then our contention is vain. That Text can be Traditional only if it goes back **without break or intermission to the original autographs**, because if through break or intermission it ceased or failed to exist, it loses the essential feature of genuine tradition...I claim to have **proved Dr. Hort to have been conspicuously wrong, and our maintenance of the Traditional Text in unbroken succession to be eminently right."**[65] [HDW, my emphasis]

Furthermore, the evidence provided by the narrow route is overwhelming from two aspects:

1. the variety of distinguishing witnesses (MSS, church elders, lectionaries, and multiple language versions), and
2. the wide geographical distribution. The manuscripts (MSS) from God's route vary just enough to affirm that they go back to the originals through many independent sources; whereas the corrupter's route manuscripts are filled with multiple defacing of the MSS, MSS cast aside and of poor quality, and MSS with evidence of cultic influences.

The documentation for this will not be provided here. It is widely available in MANY books, articles, and internet sites.

---

[64] Neologian is the term coined by Dean Burgon and Edward Miller for the Alexandrian or 'new' Greek text constructed by textual critics that culminated with Westcott and Hort.

[65] Dean John William Burgon, *The Causes of Corruption of the Traditional Text of the Holy Gospels Being the Sequel to the Traditional Text of the Holy Gospels, Vol. II* (Dean Burgon Society Press, Collingswood, NJ, 1896, reprinted 1998) 1-3.

"The one great Fact, which especially troubles him [HORT] and his joint Editor [WESTCOTT],—(as well it may)—is *The Traditional Greek Text* of the New Testament Scriptures. Call this Text <u>Erasmian</u> or <u>Complutensian,</u>—the Text of <u>Stephens</u>, or of <u>Beza</u>, or of the <u>Elzevirs,</u>—call it the '<u>Received,</u>' or *Traditional Greek Text*, or <u>whatever other name you please;</u>—the fact remains, that a Text *has* come down to us which is attested by a general consensus of ancient Copies, ancient Fathers, ancient Versions."[66]

In his book, *The Traditional Text of the Holy Gospels*, Burgon said:

"Variety distinguishing witness massed together must needs constitute a most powerful argument for believing such Evidence to be true. Witnesses of different kinds; from different countries; speaking different tongues:--witnesses who can never have met, and between whom it is incredible that there should exist collusion of any kind:--such witnesses deserve to be listened to most respectfully. Indeed, when witnesses of so varied a sort agree in large numbers, they must needs be accounted worthy of even implicit confidence... Variety it is which imparts virtue to mere Number, prevents the witness-box from being filled with packed deponents, ensures genuine testimony. False witness is thus detected and condemned, because it agrees not with the rest. Variety is the consent of independent witnesses,...

It is precisely this consideration which constrains us to pay supreme attention to the combined testimony of the Uncials and of the whole body of the Cursive Copies. They are (a) dotted over at least 1000 years: (b) they evidently [Burgon means by evidence, there is no doubt here, HDW] belong to so many divers countries,—Greece, Constantinople, Asia Minor, Palestine, Syria, Alexandria, and other part of Africa, not to say Sicily, Southern Italy, Gaul, England and Ireland: (c) they exhibit so many strange characteristics and peculiar sympathies: (d) they so clearly represent countless families of MSS., being in no single instance absolutely

---

[66] Dean John William Burgon, *The Revision Revised* (The Dean Burgon Society Press, Collingswood, NJ, originally published, 1883, reprinted 2000) 269.

identical in their text, and certainly not being copies of any
other Codex in existence,--that their unanimous decision I
hold to be an absolutely irrefragable evidence of the Truth."[67]
[my addition, HDW]

A Hollow Claim

What is the hollow claim that the Words *received* cannot be
determined without further discoveries of old manuscripts, when God
promised their availability from generation to generation *"for ever"*? We
have the Words. We have had them all along. The Traditional Texts of the
Holy Scripture were brought together by God's providential care. The
Words found underlying the King James Bible are the Words of God
preserved throughout the centuries. They are the Words found in the
majority of manuscripts that are virtually identical and that can easily be
collated:

(1) from lectionaries,

(2) from various ancient language versions, and

(3) from church elder writings.

The Words were compiled by the expertise of men providentially
brought together in the early sixteen hundreds to establish finally the
preservation of God's Words. The scholarship and linguistic abilities of
the KJB translators has never been matched.

Surely, the providence of God was related to:

(1) the abilities of these men,

(2) the invention of the printing press in the 15th century, and

(3) its rapid improvement over the next two centuries.

God wanted the inspired Words preserved from His ordained route
ready for wide distribution as a result of:

[67] Dean John William Burgon, *The Traditional Text of the Holy Gospels, Vol
1* (The Dean Burgon Society Press, Collingswood, NJ, 1998) 50-51.

(1) the printing press,

(2) the explosion of population, and

(3) the geographical expansion of nations into the 'new' regions, particularly the Americas.

There is no indication in Scripture that He would preserve His Words by hiding them:

(1) in graves,

(2) at the Vatican library on a shelf, or

(3) in other various dark and nefarious places.

In fact, He repeatedly indicates in Scripture that they would be readily available as already demonstrated. They would not be secret, hidden, or across the ocean (i.e. hard to get to or find). Wouldn't manuscripts buried in the sands of Egypt in graves and garbage dumps qualify as hidden?

Furthermore, the availability of the Words of God to **ALL** can certainly be demonstrated. In many geographical areas of the known world during the immediate post-apostolic era, readily available copies of God's Words were corrupted, particularly in Alexandria, Egypt. These manuscripts demonstrate that the cults, the apostates, and the heretics applied their penknives to them very early in the Church Age to make them compatible with their philosophies. The churches recognized the corrupted manuscripts and refused to use them. This accounts for the preservation of many corrupted manuscripts that were not RECEIVED. They were not used. They were placed in the "back room" on a shelf and were occasionally used by monks as material to be burned in order to keep warm. This is precisely how Tischendorf found the Sinaiticus manuscript named Aleph at St. Catherine's Monastery in the Sinai desert. The Monks were burning Aleph to keep warm because it had been determined to be corrupted and of little use. A few variations of the corrupted Aleph manuscript such as B, Beza, A (Alexandrinus), and about 40+ others have been discovered. This is a paltry number compared to the overwhelming number of *Traditional/Received* type Greek manuscripts that number more than 5,000. This number does not include the vast amount of other language versions of the Bible and church father writings that support the Words behind the King James Bible. The most favorite manuscript used by the most infamous corrupters, WH, is manuscript B.

Many False Claims (Theories) Have Been Refuted

Individuals making many false claims and proposing speculative theories are in opposition to the Lord Jesus Christ's COMMAND to *receive* God's preserved Words and their AFTs. They have been refuted repeatedly by evidence from Scripture and from history. For example, consider the following false claims in no particular order:

(1) There are hundreds of thousands of errors in the God-ordained route manuscripts,

(2) There was hasty collation of the Received Texts/Traditional Texts (RT/TT) by Erasmus in order to rush to publication the first printed edition,

(3) There are readings in the texts behind the KJB that are not found in any manuscripts,

(4) There are verses included in Erasmus' Greek RT text editions secondary to promises by Erasmus related to finding one MSS with the Words (i.e. 1 Jn. 5:7),

(5) The differences between the RT/TT and the Critical Text (CT) are minor,

(6) There are multiple incorrect words in the KJB translation such as "strain at a gnat,"

(7)   There are over 8,000 marginal notes related to textual criticism in the KJB,

(8)   The KJB was a provisional translation,

(9)   There have been 100,000 changes over the years in the KJB,

(10)   Many of the RT/TT readings were created by conflation by overzealous scribes,

(11)   The RT/TT readings are late due to recensions,

(12)   The KJB translation is hard to read and is outdated due to "Elizabethan" language such as thee, thy, thou, ye, etc.,

(13)   "The oldest and best" MSS are those discarded for 1500 years, which have been located in the Vatican, graves and garbage dumps in Egypt, and garbage cans in Monasteries,

(14)   The "received text" (textus receptus) (RT) began with Erasmus, and

(15)   **many** similar claims.

They are all wrong. God's Words refute many of their claims in many passages, but:

> "...they obeyed not, neither inclined their ear, but made their neck stiff, that they might not hear, nor **receive** instruction" (Jeremiah 17:23).

Furthermore, claims such as those above are repeatedly answered and corrected by scholarly men such as:

(1) the KJB translators,

(2) the author H.J. de Jonge, the Dean of the Faculty of Theology at Rijksuniversiteit (Leiden, Netherlands),

(3) Dr. Herman Hoskier (foremost manuscript scholar, particularly on the book of Revelation),

(4) Dr. Edward Hills (Yale, Westminster, Columbia trained textual critic),

(5) Dr. D. A. Waite (foremost Hebrew/Greek/Latin linguist and KJB/RT/TT/Burgon scholar),

(6) Dr. Jack Moorman (foremost manuscript scholar), and

(7) many other experts and students of God's Words such as Dr. Jeffery Khoo (Dean, Far Eastern Bible College) and Dr. David Cloud (self-taught KJB/RT/TT/CT history and text scholar).

Yet, the CT proponents continue to copy one another and repeat the same old claims and errors because they cannot **receive** the Words of God, preserved, pure, perfect, protected, and provided to us by the nation Israel and the sanctified churches that were filled with the priesthood of believers. They know if they do *receive* the Words that they will have to come under the **authority** of the precise message provided by the precise Words. Absolute authority is a very objectionable proposition and reality for the postmodernist.

An Example

For example, Dr. Jack Moorman corrected Dr. Daniel Wallace, a Greek professor at Dallas Theological Seminary, for repeating the very common claim that there are numerous errors in all of the manuscripts. However, Dr. Wallace fails to point out that the majority of errors are in a handful of manuscripts (less than 50). The MSS of the majority, RT, TT, route are virtually identical. They are the manuscripts behind the KJB. Dr. Moorman said:

> "Again Wallace says: 'There are over 400,000 textual variants among the N.T. manuscripts. But the differences between the Textus Receptus and the texts based on the best Greek witnesses number about 5000." Had he gone to

the trouble, he would have tacitly revealed a very uncomfortable fact for his position. A hugely disproportionate amount of the variation is to be found among the relatively few manuscripts supporting the Aleph-B text. The critical editors, Barbara Aland and Klaus Wachtel admit this:

> 'The papyri and majuscules are for the most part individual witnesses: despite sharing general tendencies on the forms of their texts, they differ so widely from one another that it is impossible to establish and direct genealogical ties among them.' ("The Greek Minuscule Manuscripts of the N.T.", *The text of the N.T. in Contemporary Research*. P. 46)

If these few cannot agree among themselves, then how can Wallace call them the "best Greek witness"? As so little of an Aleph-B kind of manuscript is available, clearly early scribes did not think them best. Nor did the scribes of the 8th/9th Centuries think them best when they transferred the text from uncial to minuscule script."[68]

Another False Claim

Also, there is another claim that is often repeated. Dean Burgon believed the Greek **Received** Text needed some more work in a few places, which is true. However, this does not negate his recognition that the Traditional Text behind the King James Bible is the exact Words of the original MSS (autographs) (see the following quote and his quote below).

> "First, be it understood, that we do not advocate perfection in the Textus Receptus. We allow that here and there it requires revision...What we maintain is the TRADITIONAL TEXT. And we trace it back to the earliest ages of which there is any record."[69]

---

[68] Dr. Jack Moorman, "A Reply to Dr. Daniel Wallace's 'Why I Do Not Think the King James Bible is the Best Translation Available Today,' Twenty Points of Criticism Answered" (http://www.biblefortoday.org/Articles/reply.htm).

[69] Dean John William Burgon, *The Traditional Text of the Holy Gospels, Volume I* (Dean Burgon Society Press, Collingswood, NJ, originally published in 1896 by his assistant Edward Miller, 1998) 5.

The Traditional Text varies from Beza's Received Text in 190 places. Most of them are very **insignificant**. Dr. Edward F. Hills, a scholar trained at Yale, Columbia, and Westminster, lists a few (9) of the most significant differences in the Received Texts in his book, *The King James Version Defended*. He proceeds then to say:

> "This comparison indicates that the differences which distinguish the various editions of the Textus Receptus from each other are very minor. They are also very few…The texts of the several editions of the Textus Receptus were God-guided. They were set up under the leading of God's special providence…But what do we do in these few places in which the several editions of the Textus Receptus disagree with one another? Which text do we follow? The answer to this question is easy. We are guided by the common faith. Hence we favor that form of the Textus Receptus upon which more than any other God, working providentially, has placed the stamp of His approval, namely, the King James Version, or, more precisely, the Greek text underlying the King James Version."[70]

In the eighteen eighties, Dean Burgon asked Dr. Frederick H. A. Scrivener to publish the Greek Text behind the KJB. It is 98% Beza's 1598 RT edition of the *received* Greek text and a few places (190) were discovered to come from other RT editions of Erasmus and Stephanus and other documents.[71] The incredible KJB translators and scholars were providentially brought together by God's guiding hand for the task of placing the exact Words in one place at such a time as that.

We believe, trust, accept, and Biblically *receive* that those very Words are the exact Words God desires us to

---

[70] Edward F. Hills, *The King James Version Defended* (The Christian Research Press, Des Moines, Iowa, 4th Edition, Reprint 1993) 222-223.
[71] Dr. Frederick H. A. Scrivener, *Scrivener's Annotated Greek New Testament, Being the Exact Greek Textus Receptus That Underlies the King James Bible* (Dean Burgon Society Press, Collingswood, NJ, 1999) ix.

have by faith; we believe they are the exact Words of the original inspired Words recorded by the Apostles and prophets. They are the exact Words God promised to preserve for us (Psa. 12:6-7, Mat. 4:4, 24:35, 1 Pe. 1:23-25).

The Critical Text (CT) route has the equivalent of the entire books of Jude and Revelation missing in comparison to the Greek Received Text (RT). Dr. Jack Moorman has recorded the 8,000 differences between the RT and the CT.[72] We will not surrender to the proponents of the CT route, because we have *received* the preserved Words and we have refused the words constructed by men. The critical text people are still searching for the Words. Dean John William Burgon believed:

"He who surrenders the first page of his Bible, surrenders **all**."[73] "The express Revelation of the Eternal is that whereon Theological Science builds her fabric of imperishable Truth: that fabric which, while other modes change, shift, and at last become superseded, shines out,-- yea, and to the very end of Time will shine out,--unconscious of decay, incapable of improvement, far, far beyond the reach of fashion: a thing unchanged, because in its very nature unchangeable!"[74]

We will not surrender one Word or one page to the textual critics. We believe God.

---

[72] Dr. Jack Moorman, *8,000 Differences Between the Textus Receptus and the Nestle-Aland NT Greek Texts* (The Bible For Today Press and The Dean Burgon Society Press, Collingswood, NJ, 2006). The Nestle-Aland Text is virtually identical to the United Bible Society Greek text. They are in the *Critical Text* (CT) families.

[73] Dean John William Burgon, *Inspiration and Interpretation* (Dean Burgon Society Press, Collingswood, NJ, originally published 1861, 1999) 50.

[74] Ibid. 120 (Burgon, *Inspiration and Interpretation*).

Blind Guides

Those who are continually straining "*at a gnat*" are truly "*blind guides*" that will have to stand at the judgment seat of Christ and explain their actions for discouraging so many and helping to create the philosophical *uncertainty* sweeping the world called postmodernism (Mat. 23:24, 2 Cor. 5:10). Surely, they fear; surely, they understand "*the terror of the Lord*" (2 Cor. 5:11). They have contributed immensely to the failure of the church in this dispensation by creating confusion, specifically confusion about the Words of God. The many and varied wordings in the 'new' versions would cause anyone to be confused who had not spent untold hours, like this author has, resolving the issues that the enemy has wrought. Shame on those who have participated in the critical text folly! (Phil. 3:17-19) May God have mercy on your souls! You have discouraged at best, or prevented at worst, many from *receiving* His glorious Words that light the world with **certainty** (Pro. 22:21). The receiving of God's Words and the personal protecting and guarding of them by born-again believers is a commandment not only put forth in the New Testament, but repeatedly and forcibly stated in the Old Testament.

The Old Testament Commands
Receiving His Words

> "*Moreover he said unto me, Son of man, **all my words** that I shall speak unto thee **receive** in thine heart, and hear with thine ears*"(Ezekiel 3:10).

The act of *receiving* God's Words is clearly revealed in Words written for us in the Old Testament, which the Apostle Paul affirmed are for our admonition and learning (1 Cor. 10:6, Rom. 15:4, Lk. 24:27). Moses went "*into the mount*" to "*receive*" the tables God had written with

His own finger (Deut. 9:9). God wrote them. Moses was to *receive* them. This is the act of receiving, which every blood-bought believer must do with the Words of God. The book of Proverbs constantly reminds us to perceive (or discern) and *receive*, wisdom, understanding, judgments, discernment, and His commandments. For example,

> *"To know wisdom and instruction; to perceive the words of understanding; To* **receive** *the instruction of wisdom, justice, and judgment, and equity"* (Proverbs 1:2-3). *"***Receive** *my instruction, and not silver; and knowledge rather than choice gold"* (Proverbs 8:10). *"The wise in heart will* **receive** *commandments: but a prating fool shall fall"* (Proverbs 10:8). *"When the scorner is punished, the simple is made wise: and when the wise is instructed, he* **receiveth** *knowledge"* (Proverbs 21:11). *"In vain have I smitten your children; they* **received** *no correction: your own sword hath devoured your prophets, like a destroying lion"* (Jeremiah 2:30, cf. 5:3, 7:28, 17:23). *"Yet hear the word of the LORD, O ye women, and let your ear* **receive** *the word of his mouth, and teach your daughters wailing, and every one her neighbour lamentation"* (Jeremiah 9:20). *"She obeyed not the voice; she* **received** *not correction; she trusted not in the LORD; she drew not near to her God"* (Zephaniah 3:2).

The Hebrew word rendered *receive* in these verses is לקח (laqach), which is very similar in meaning to the Greek word, λαμβανω (lambanō). It suggests that we are to "accept", "seize", and "take hold of" or "latch onto." This means not only to discern His Words and keep them in our hearts, but we are to understand that they came from His lips; they are His voice. Furthermore, we are to "*keep*" (preserve) them, which is discussed below.

Over the years, this author has received some gifts that are priceless in terms of the thought behind the gift, but not in the value of the object. While on mission trips to countries such as Hungary, Chile, Mexico, etc., gifts were given to this author on his departure from those he had ministered to, that were only pennies in cost, but priceless in terms of their significance. The people were poor and could barely afford food on their tables. Giving any gift, even though it was inexpensive, placed a strain on them. The thought always came to mind of the widow's two mites (Lk. 21:2-3). Just as God received the widow's gift with rejoicing, this author with rejoicing received the gifts from the poor. Have you received God's gift of His precise, preserved, inspired Words, which contain His thoughts, with rejoicing and thanksgiving?

Words, in and of themselves, whether spoken or written, are not worth much (Ecc. 7:21). Unless the source of the Words is from the One who fulfilled the Beatitudes perfectly, who was without sin, who proved His Being (He was the *"I am"*) with amazing knowledge and miracles, and who gave His life for our redemption to prove His love. He reversed the curse of sin and death. This is the One who is waiting to receive those who believe on Him into mansions in glory *"for ever."* This is the One whose Words are absolute Truth. The benefits of receiving His Words cannot be exhausted. They are innumerable. A few will be outlined from the Scripture.

The Benefits of Receiving His Words

"So then faith cometh by hearing, and hearing by the word of God" (Romans 10:17).

What a great benefit from receiving God's Words by faith. God's Word(s) of Truth that point to the Lord Jesus Christ and the completed work on the Cross bring about salvation by grace through faith. Furthermore, His Words:

1.   cause conviction of our sin,
2.   cause confession of our sin, and

3. cause us to repent of our sin.

The Words:

4. convince us of His love for us and

5. constrain us to obey.

They bring about:

6. creation of a new man,

7. confidence in His Words,

8. consecration to Him, and

9. care for His flock with love and diligence.

All of these things come by simply believing, trusting, and *receiving* Him and His Words as absolute Truth. But wait, there is more. His Words declare that:

1. We receive the atonement (Rom. 5:11).

2. We are reconciled to God (2 Cor. 5:18-19).

3. We are freed from bondage (Rom. 8:15).

4. We receive the adoption as children of God (Rom. 8:15).

5. We receive one another (Rom. 15:7).

6. We receive the Spirit of God (Rom. 8:15).

7. We receive the Words of the prophets (Mat. 10:41).

8. We receive seed on the good ground (Mat. 13:23).

9. We receive everlasting life (Mat. 19:29).

10. We receive whatsoever we ask of Him in prayer according to His will (Mat. 21:22, Mk. 11:24, Jn. 16:24).

11. We will receive a hundred fold for giving up the lust of the world, eyes, and flesh (Mk. 10:30).

12. We receive His fullness and grace (Jn. 1:16).

13. We receive nothing save it be given to us from heaven (Jn. 3:27).

14. We receive all of His promises (Jn. 3:33).

15. We receive freedom from judgment by His Words (Jn. 12:47-48, 1 Jn. 1:9).

16. We receive Him and the Father if we receive those He sends (Jn. 13:20).

17. We receive the Holy Spirit who dwells with us and we shall know Him (Jn 14:27, Acts 2:38).

18. We receive His Words given to the Holy Spirit from the Lord Jesus Christ and the Father (Jn. 16:24,   ).

19. We will receive joy (Jn. 16:24).

20. We shall receive power to be witnesses (Acts 1:8).

21. We are received as a people for his name (Acts 15:14).

22. We receive forgiveness of our sins (Acts 26:18).

23. We receive sight (Acts 26:18).

24. We receive the inheritance of Christ (Acts 26:18).

25. We receive protection from the power of Satan (Acts 26:18).

26. We receive the Words and become followers of the Lord with joy of the Holy Spirit (often in much affliction from the world) (1 Thess. 1:6);

27. and many other promises.

His Received Words Work Effectually

*"For this cause also thank we God without ceasing, because, when ye **received** the word of God which ye heard of us, ye received it not as the word of men, but as it is in truth, **the word of God, which effectually worketh** also in you that believe." (1 Thess. 2:13).*

In a Sunday morning message on 10/21/07, Pastor D. A. Waite listed the following benefits for receiving the Words of God, which effectually work in the believer:

(1) TO LEARN WHAT IS "RIGHT"
   Psalm 33:4
   For the word of the LORD is right; and all his works are done in truth. (KJV)

(2) TO CLEANSE US
   Psalm 119:9
   BETH. Wherewithal shall a young man cleanse his way? by taking heed *thereto* according to thy word. (KJV)

(3) TO PREVENT OUR SINNING
   Psalm 119:11
   Thy word have I hid in mine heart, that I might not sin against thee. (KJV)

(4) TO QUICKEN US [GIVE US LIFE]
   Psalm 119:25
   DALETH. My soul cleaveth unto the dust: quicken thou me according to thy word. (KJV)
   Philippians 2:16
   Holding forth the word of life; that I may rejoice in the day of Christ, that I have not run in vain, neither laboured in vain. (KJV)

(5) TO STRENGTHEN US
   Psalm 119:28
   My soul melteth for heaviness: strengthen thou me according unto thy word. (KJV)

(6) TO GIVE US HOPE
   Psalm 119:49
   ZAIN. Remember the word unto thy servant, upon which thou hast caused me to hope. (KJV)

(7) TO COMFORT US
   Psalm 119:50
   This *is* my comfort in my affliction: for thy word hath quickened me. (KJV)

(8) TO KEEP US FROM GOING ASTRAY
Psalm 119:67
  Before I was afflicted I went astray: but now have I kept thy word. (KJV)

(9) TO KEEP US FROM EVIL WAYS
Psalm 119:101
  I have refrained my feet from every evil way, that I might keep thy word. (KJV)

(10) TO LIGHT OUR FEET AND PATH
Psalm 119:105
  Thy word *is* a lamp unto my feet, and a light unto my path. (KJV)

(11) TO KEEP US FROM INIQUITY
Psalm 119:133
  Order my steps in thy word: and let not any iniquity have dominion over me. (KJV)

(12) TO KEEP US FROM TRANSGRESSIONS
Psalm 119:158
  I beheld the transgressors, and was grieved; because they kept not thy word. (KJV)

(13) TO BRING US REJOICING
Psalm 119:162
  I rejoice at thy word, as one that findeth great spoil. (KJV)

(14) TO GIVE US UNDERSTANDING
Psalm 119:169
  Let my cry come near before thee, O LORD: give me understanding according to thy word. (KJV)

(15) TO SANCTIFY US
John 17:17
  Sanctify them through thy truth: thy word is truth. (KJV)
Ephesians 5:26
  That he might sanctify and cleanse it with the washing of water by the word, (KJV)

(16) TO BUILD US UP
Acts 20:32

And now, brethren, <u>I commend you to God, and to the word of his grace, which is able to build you up, and to give you an inheritance among all them which are sanctified</u>. (KJV)

(17) TO GIVE US FAITH
Romans 10:17
So then <u>faith cometh by hearing, and hearing by the word of God</u>. (KJV)

(18) TO GIVE US RECONCILIATION
2 Corinthians 5:19
To wit, that <u>God was in Christ, reconciling the world unto himself, not imputing their trespasses unto them; and hath committed unto us the word of reconciliation. (KJV)</u>

(19) TO GIVE US THE SWORD OF THE SPIRIT
Ephesians 6:17
And <u>take the helmet of salvation, and the sword of the Spirit, which is the word of God</u>: (KJV)

(20) TO NOURISH US
1 Timothy 4:6
If thou put the brethren in remembrance of these things, thou shalt be a good minister of Jesus Christ, <u>nourished up in the words of faith and of good doctrine</u>, whereunto thou hast attained. (KJV)

(21) TO GIVE US SOMETHING TO PREACH
2 Timothy 4:2
<u>Preach the word</u>; be instant in season, out of season; reprove, rebuke, exhort with all longsuffering and doctrine. (KJV)

(22) TO CONVINCE THE GAINSAYERS
Titus 1:9
<u>Holding fast the faithful word</u> as he hath been taught, that he may be able by sound doctrine both to exhort and <u>to convince the gainsayers</u>. (KJV)

(23) TO GIVE US SOMETHING POWERFUL
Hebrews 4:12
<u>For the word of God is quick, and powerful</u>, and sharper than any twoedged sword, piercing even to the dividing

asunder of soul and spirit, and of the joints and marrow, and is a discerner of the thoughts and intents of the heart. (KJV)

(24) TO GIVE US RIGHTEOUSNESS
Hebrews 5:13
For every one that useth milk is unskilful in the word of righteousness: for he is a babe. (KJV)

(25) TO BEGET US AS HIS CHILDREN AND SAVE US
James 1:18
Of his own will begat he us with the word of truth, that we should be a kind of firstfruits of his creatures. (KJV)
James 1:21
Wherefore lay apart all filthiness and superfluity of naughtiness, and receive with meekness the engrafted word, which is able to save your souls. (KJV)
1 Peter 1:23
Being born again, not of corruptible seed, but of incorruptible, by the word of God, which liveth and abideth for ever. (KJV)

(26) TO GIVE THE BASIS OF THE GOSPEL TO PREACH
1 Peter 1:25
But the word of the Lord endureth for ever. And this is the word which by the gospel is preached unto you. (KJV)

(27) TO GIVE US GROWTH
1 Peter 2:2
As newborn babes, desire the sincere milk of the word, that ye may grow thereby: (KJV)

(28) TO GIVE US ACCURATE PROPHECY
2 Peter 1:19
We have also a more sure word of prophecy; whereunto ye do well that ye take heed, as unto a light that shineth in a dark place, until the day dawn, and the day star arise in your hearts: (KJV)"

The problem is that most men question or corrupt His Words by changing, adding, or subtracting from them instead of simply *receiving* the Words with joy and thankfulness. In his translator's notes to the Confessions of St. Augustine, J. G. Pilkington characterized the age of

Augustine, and the characterization could be applied to the recent centuries:

> "It was an age in which there was action and reaction between religion and philosophy; but in which the power of Christianity was so great in its influences on Paganism, that some received the Christian Scriptures **only to embody in their phraseology the ideas of heathenism**."[75] [my emphasis, HDW]

In the last several decades, the influence of Christianity has fallen by the wayside. The root cause is the refusal of many men who are called by His name to *receive* God's Words. The cause of the uncertainty is generated by the endless "digging" for and **reconstruction** of God's Words by modernistic textual critics, which results in further corruption, doubt, and dismay for the many innocent souls who are so confused by all of the malarkey and ilk published and presented in these last days.

God said:

> *"I said, Surely thou wilt fear me, thou wilt **receive** instruction; so their dwelling should not be cut off, howsoever I punished them: but they rose early, and **corrupted** all their doings"* (Zephaniah 3:7).

Why not simply *receive* and *keep* His Words, which have been preserved from generation to generation, faith to faith, and sanctified church to sanctified church? They are the ways of life, the paths of a just man, the protection everyone seeks, and the need of every man. However, what is often overlooked is the way and the responsibility God has commanded to *keep* His Words from corruption. The responsibility to keep them is increasingly shunned because precise authoritative Words

---

[75] J. G. Pilkington, "The Confessions of St. Augustine," (*Translator's Notes, The Master Christian Library,* Rio, WI, Ages Software, Ver. 8, 2000.) 46.

are rejected and the message from them 'generalized.' The Words become simply an indefinite message or concept. What is forgotten is that God's precise, preserved, pure words form the message; and if the words are changed, the message changes.

Keeping His Words or Being Nicolaitans

> *"He that hath my commandments, and **keepeth** them, he it is that loveth me: and he that loveth me shall be loved of my Father, and I will love him, and will manifest myself to him" (John 14:21) "Jesus answered and said unto him, If a man love me, he will **keep** my **words**: and my Father will love him, and we will come unto him, and make our abode with him." (John 14:23)*

There is an important difference in the doctrine to *"keep"* His Words as opposed to "do" or *"obey"* His Words. It is often missed. The following verse gives us insight into the significance and the importance God attributes to *"keeping"* His Words. It is not the usual interpretation everyone hears from the pulpit or reads in books or articles because the meaning has been lost.

> *"And whatsoever we ask, we receive of him, because we **keep** his commandments, and **do** those things that are pleasing in his sight"* (1 John 3:22). (The NIV and NLT use obey here, also)

What we generally hear from pastors, teachers and missionaries is the explanation that "**keep**" means simply "obey" in the verse above. As we shall see, this is wrong.

There are different Hebrew and Greek words used in the OT and the NT for "obey" and "do" as opposed to "keep." The words have different meanings.

The Often Missed Meaning of "Keep" in the OT and NT

This topic has been addressed very carefully and academically in a book by several men, *Thou Shalt Keep Them,* Kent Brandenburg, Editor. It is a scholarly work, which outlines the often missed meaning of *"keep"* in the Old and New Testaments. The disciples of the Lord in the OT and NT understood the meaning. It appears over the years the meaning has been mollified or completely lost by most students of God's Words. Perhaps it has been neglected because of the disdain for the truth of preservation and for the method of preservation of the Scriptures by so many individuals in the last several hundred years. Also, it may well be related to the increasing tendency of man to reject personal responsibility for anything. This brief work cannot cover all the details. But the important concept for the believer today is that when the Lord Jesus Christ, or the prophets and Apostles spoke or recorded the Hebrew words, shamar and natsar, or the Greek word, tereo, or their cognates, which often underlies the English word, *"keep,"* in the OT and NT, it generally meant something far different than the semantic meaning used today.

Let us examine the "Great Commission" which is the commandment by our Lord to the churches:

> *"Go ye therefore, and teach all nations, baptizing them in the name of the Father, and of the Son, and of the Holy Ghost: Teaching them to **observe** all things whatsoever I have commanded you: and, lo, I am with you alway, even unto the end of the world." Amen"* (Matthew 28:19-20).

The Greek word behind "observe" is a present, active infinitive, terein, from the root word, tereo, which means to:

*"keep in view, take note, **watch over**; (1) literally; (a)
guard (AC 12.6); (b) keep, hold in reserve, **preserve** for a
purpose or until a suitable time (JN 2.10); ... c)
maintain, keep (JU 6a), opposite of πόλλυμι (forfeit, lose);
(d) protect, keep intact, keep inviolate (1C 7.37); (2)
figuratively; (a) spiritually, of persons **guard, preserve,
protect** (JN 17.11); (b) as maintaining the essence of the*
Christian life *keep* (2T 4.7); (c) with reference to doctrine,
commandments, precepts *observe, obey* [76]

If one takes all of the suggested meanings into account, the usual
preaching, teaching, or writing proclaimed today neglects many of these
concepts: to *"guard, preserve for a purpose or until a suitable time, keep
intact, protect."* Could this be a *"Nicolaitan"* tendency, which is the trend
to "lord over" or "rule over" others by the tradition of man (Rev. 2:15)?
Could this be the influence of the modern versions? (see the NIV and NLT
at Jn. 14:15 which translate the word behind "keep" in the KJB as "obey";
see below).

Surely, the disciples understood the other meanings of the Greek
word behind "keep," since Greek was the language used to record God's
Words. Furthermore, surely they instructed those added to the church
during their time about these things. Surely, some of those added to the
church were priests that were scribes skilled in making copies to "keep"
the inspired Words..[77] Therefore, the inspired writings were skillfully
copied immediately and often because they were in demand.

Furthermore, the Apostles and prophets experienced the process
of inspiration. They knew at once that the Words they recorded were from

---

[76] Timothy Friberg, Friberg, Barbara ; Miller, Neva F. (*Analytical Lexicon of
the Greek New Testament*, Baker Books, Grand Rapids, Mich., 2000, Baker's
Greek New Testament Library 4), S. 379

[77] The priests added to the apostolic church were often skilled as scribes. They
would be able to impart strict instructions to the early church for making
copies. (See Acts 6:7, which says: *"a great company of the priests were
obedient to the faith."*

God[78] (see footnote 20). They encouraged copies of the Words to be made immediately for other churches because they understood God's command to "keep" them with extreme care and diligence (e.g. Rev. 1:11). The meticulousness matched the extreme care and diligence of the OT scribes.[79] The prophets and scribes understood God's command to "keep" His Words (e.g. Jn. 14:15, 21-23).

Understanding the Command to Keep His Words

In the book of Revelation, the Apostle John was told to record the Words given to him and to send them to the seven churches (Rev. 1:11, 19). How could this be done unless exact copies (as humanly possible)

---

[78] Paul makes it clear that there were MANY corrupters immediately, saying: For we are not as many, which corrupt the word of God: but as of sincerity, but as of God, in the sight of God speak we in Christ. (2 Corinthians 2:17, the 'new' versions often corrupt this verse for obvious reasons; they wrongly use the word "peddle" instead of "corrupt"). There were frauds (con men) as well. Paul recorded: "That ye be not soon shaken in mind, or be troubled, neither by spirit, nor by word, nor by letter as from us, as that the day of Christ is at hand" (2 Thessalonians 2:2). However, the knowledge of the inspired texts (i.e. which ones were inspired) was known to the church even before the Apostles passed on to glory. For example, Peter reports Paul's letters were inspired: "And account that the longsuffering of our Lord is salvation; even as our beloved brother Paul also according to the wisdom given unto him hath written unto you; As also in all his epistles, speaking in them of these things; in which are some things hard to be understood, which they that are unlearned and unstable wrest, as they do also the other scriptures, unto their own destruction" (2 Peter 3:15-16). Paul knew Luke's writings were inspired, quoting as Scripture a phrase found only in Luke: "For the scripture saith, Thou shalt not muzzle the ox that treadeth out the corn. And, The labourer is worthy of his reward" (1 Timothy 5:18). The labourer is worthy of his reward is found only in Lk. 10:7 (i.e. same Greek words, not exactly same English words).

[79] Pastor D. A. Waite, Th.D., Ph.D., *Defending the King James Bible* (Bible For Today Press, Collingswood, NJ, 8th printing, 2002) 24-26.

were made? Did they not follow the commands of the Lord concerning preserving His Words? Surely the commands recorded by John's gospel were ringing in the ears of believers in Ephesus and beyond:

> *"If ye love me, **keep** (Gr. tereo) my commandments"* (John 14:15). *"He that hath my commandments, and **keepeth** (Gr. tereo) them, he it is that loveth me: and he that loveth me shall be loved of my Father, and I will love him, and will manifest myself to him"* (John 14:21). *"If ye **keep** (Gr. tereo) my commandments, ye shall abide in my love; even as I have **kept** (Gr. tereo) my Father's commandments, and abide in his love"* (John 15:10). *"And shewing mercy unto thousands of them that love me and **keep** (Heb. shamar) my commandments"* (Deut. 5:10; cf. 1 Tim. 6:20, 2 Tim. 1:14, 1 Jn 2:3, 5:3, Rev. 1:3, 3:10, 12:17, 22:19, Ex 16:28; 20:6; Le 22:31; 26:3; De 5:10,29; 1Ki 3:14; 6:12; 9:6; 11:38; 2Ki 17:13; 1Ch 29:19; Ne 1:9; Ps 89:31; 119:115; Pr 3:1; 4:4; 7:1-2; Da 9:4) (my additions and emphasis, HDW).

Do you believe that born-again members of sanctified churches throughout the centuries would add to or conflate, remove, or change the Words given by our Lord? This author does not. Certainly, they made a few unintentional scribal errors, but not much else. This is the reason the copies are virtually identical from MANY countries and MANY sources.

Even Augustine of Hippo, who was a progenitor of allegorical hermeneutics and the father of the Roman Catholic Church extolled **receiving** the Words of God. Augustine wrote to a fellow believer and her daughter, saying:

> "…our humble ministry also was of use to you, for when you had **received the word of God** from us, "**you received it**," as says the apostle, "not as the word of men, but as it is in truth the word of God."[80] (my emphasis, HDW)

---

[80] Augustine, "To The Lady Juliana…and Her Daughter" (*Letter 188*, A. D. 416, *The Master Christian Library*, Ages Software, 2000) Chapter 1, p. 1100.

This author *receives* the Scripture as precise, preserved, permanent, protected, Words, which clearly delineate the institutions of the nation Israel and the church, who were each given the responsibility to watch over, guard, protect, and preserve His Words. The sanctified institutions were made up of believing individuals who understood that their faith in God was accompanied by certain responsibilities. There is overwhelming evidence that they did exactly as they were commanded and as we are commanded today.

The Bereans demonstrated the act of receiving the Scriptures as the Words of God because they recognized the Words had been "kept." The Bereans:

> "...were more noble than those in Thessalonica, in that they **received** the word with all readiness of mind, and searched the scriptures daily, whether those things were so" (Acts 17:11).

This author cannot fathom that any believer seeking to please and serve the Lord Jesus Christ, would turn to or use a 'bible' that is the result of a route plagued by:

1. **c**orruption,
2. infected by **c**ults and
3. **c**on men,
4. who deny the **c**hronological
5. **p**resence (availability),
6. **p**urity, and
7. **p**reservation of the Scripture found in the *received* traditional Hebrew, Aramaic, and Greek texts available from generation to "*generation, for ever.*"

Are you *receiving* and *keeping* the Words of our Lord as COMMANDED?

BIBLIOGRAPHY

Augustine. "Questions of Januarius." *The Nicene and Post Nicene Fathers*, Letters of St. Augustine, Letter 55. The Master Christian Library, Ages Software, Ver. 8. 2000.
_____ "To The Lady Juliana...and Her Daughter." *Letter 188*. Rio, WI. The Master Christian Library. Ages Software, Ver. 8, 2000.

Barnes, Albert. *Albert Barnes' Notes on the Bible*. Broken Arrow, OK. SwordSearcher, Ver. 5.1.1.1. Originally published 1832-1872. 2007.

Brandenburg, Kent, Editor. *Thou Shalt Keep Them, A Biblical Theology of the Perfect Preservation of Scripture*. El Sobrante, CA. Pillar and Ground Publishing. 2003.

Burgon, Dean John William. *The Traditional Text of the Holy Gospels. Vol. 1*. Collingswood, NJ. Dean Burgon Society Press. Originally published, 1898. 1998.
_____ *The Traditional Text of the Holy Gospels.* Collingswood, NJ. Dean Burgon Society Press. Originally published, 1896. 1998.
_____ *The Causes of Corruption of the Traditional Text of* the Holy Gospels Being the Sequel to the Traditional Text of the Holy Gospels, Vol. II. Collingswood, NJ. Dean Burgon Society Press. Originally published, 1896. 1998.
_____ *Revision Revised*. Collingswood, NJ. Dean Burgon Society Press. Originally published, 1883. 2000.
_____ *Inspiration and Interpretation*. Collingswood, NJ. Dean Burgon Society Press. Originally published, 1861. 1999.

Chafer, Lewis Sperry. *Systematic Theology*. Grand Rapids, MI. Kregel Publications.

Clement of Rome. "The Epistle to the Corinthians." Rio, WI. The Master Christian Library. Ages Software, Ver. 8, 2000.

Cloud, David. "The Peerless Literary Beauty of the King James Bible." Faith vs. the Modern Bible Versions. Port Huron, MI. 2005.
_____ *Way of Life Encyclopedia*. Port Huron, MI. SwordSearcher, Version 5.1.1.1. 2007.
_____ *Things Hard to be Understood*. Port Huron, MI. Way of Life Literature. 1996.
_____ *Faith vs. the Modern Bible Versions*. Port Huron, MI. Way of Life Literature. 2005.

Edwards, Rev. Justin, and Rev. Prof. E. P. Harrows, D.D. *The Family Bible, Containing the Old and New Testament, With*

Brief Notes and Instructions. Broken Arrow, OK.
SwordSearcher, Version 5.1.1.1. First published 1861. 2007.

Friberg, Timothy ; Friberg, Barbara ; Miller, Neva F.. *Analytical Lexicon of the Greek New Testament*. Grand Rapids, Mich. Baker Books. 2000.

Fuller, David Otis. http://av1611.com/kjbp/articles/fuller-preserved.html. Accessed 10/23/07.

Gregory of Nyssa. *Against Eunomius*. The Life and Writings of Gregory of Nyssa, The Nicene and Post Nicene Fathers, The Master Christian Library, Ages Software, Ver. 8. 2000.

Hills, Edward F., *The King James Version Defended*. Des Moines, Iowa. The Christian Research Press. 4th Edition, Reprint. 1993.

Matto, Dr. Ken. "Is the King James Bible Inspired?" (accessed 11/01/07 at www.scionofzion.com/kjvinsp.htm)

Moorman, J. A. *Early Manuscripts, Church Fathers, and the Authorized Versions with Manuscript Digests and Summaries*. Collingswood, NJ. Bible For Today Press. 2005.

_____*8,000 Difference Between the Textus Receptus and the Nestle-Aland NT Greek Texts*. Collingswood, NJ. Bible For Today Press. 1990.

_____ "A Reply to Dr. Daniel Wallace's 'Why I Do Not Think the King James Bible is the Best Translation Available Today,' Twenty Points of Criticism Answered." www.biblefortoday.org/Articles/reply.htm

Packer, J. L. et al, *Translating Truth, The Case For Essentially Literal Bible Translation*. Wheaton, IL. Crossway Books. 2005.

Shafer, Pastor George. "We preach only from the pure word of God." (Accessed 10/11/07. www.odentonbaptist.org/?q=node/2.

Pilkington, J.G.. "The Confessions of St. Augustine." Rio, WI. The Master Christian Library. Ages Software, Ver. 8. 2000.

Spurgeon, C. H. "The Immutability of God—Sermon 1." *The Spurgeon Sermon Collection*. Rio, WI.. The Master Christian Library, Ages Software, Ver. 8. 2000.

_____ *Flowers From a Puritan's Garden*. Harrisonburg, VA. Sprinkle Publications. 1997.

_____ "The Bible—Sermon 15." *The Spurgeon Sermon Collection. Rio, WI.* The Master Christian Library, Ages Software. 2000.

Strouse, Thomas M. *"But My Words Shall Not Pass Away"* The Biblical Defense of the Doctrine of the Preservation of

Scripture. Newington, CT. Emmanuel Baptist Theological Press. 2001.

_____ "The Translation Model Predicted From Scripture." Newington,
   CT. Emmanuel Baptist Theological Seminary. www.emmanuel-
   newington.org/seminary/resources/KJV_Model.pdf.

Stub, J. Aall Ottesen. *Verbal Inspiration.* Decorah, Iowa. Lutheran
   Publishing House. 1915.

Sutton, Jim. "Every Word of God Proves True." (accessed
   10/11/07. www.goodwordusa.org/word/pure.htm).

Waite, Th.D., Ph.D., Dr. D. A. "Dr. Waite's Reply to Dr.
   Cassidy" (accessed 11/01/07 at:
   www.deanburgonsociety.org/DBS_Society/waite_reply.htm

_____ *The New International Version, Weighed In The*
   Balance—And Found Wanting, The N.I.V. Is Not The Word
   of God In English. Collingswood, NJ. Bible For Today Press.
   1990.

_____ *Defending the King James Bible.* Collingswood, NJ.
   Bible For Today Press. 8th printing, 2002.

Williams, H. D. *Hearing the Voice of God.* Cleveland, GA. The
   Old Paths Publications. 2008.

_____ *The Lie That Changed The Modern World.*
   Collingswood, NJ. Bible For Today Press. 2004.

_____ *Word-For-Word Translating the Received Texts,*
   Verbal Plenary Translating. Collingswood, NJ. Bible For
   Today Press. 2007.

Williams, James B., General Editor, and Randolph Shaylor,
   Managing Editor. *God's Word in Our Hands, The Bible*
   Preserved For Us. Greenville, SC. Ambassador Emerald
   International. 2003.

REFERENCE WORKS

Dean Burgon Society "Articles of Faith" www.Dean BurgonSociety.org.
Strong's Concordance
Websters 1828 Dictionary

Websites of Interest

www.theoldpathspublications.com.
www.deanburgonsociety.org.
www.biblefortoday.org

www.azom.com/Details.asp?ArticleID=2430.
www.odentonbaptist.org www.odentonbaptist.org.

INDEX

ABOUT THE AUTHOR

Dr. Williams was born in Ft. Pierce, Florida. He was saved at the age of fourteen at his local Baptist church under Pastor J. R. White where he was active in the church youth group. His local church ordained him to preach the gospel. After graduating with honors from high school, he attended Stetson University where he met his wife, Patricia, and they were married in 1961. Starting in the ministerial program at Stetson and switching to pre-med in his junior year, he graduated with honors with a B.A. After Stetson, he taught high school at Eau Gallie, Florida for two years, and then continued his training at the University of Miami Medical School where he graduated with honors. Following his medical training, Dr. Williams and Patricia settled in New Port Richey, Florida where he practiced Family Medicine as a board certified family practitioner. He was active in his community as a hospital board member for twenty years, a chief-of-staff, president of the medical society, an advisory board member and president of Moody Bible Institute's Florida program, a board member of the Health Planning Commission, and a teacher at his local Baptist church. He helped develop and administrate a multi-specialist medical clinic with forty thousand patients and seventeen doctors. His Biblical training was obtained at Stetson University, Moody Bible Institute, and Louisiana Baptist University. After retirement, Dr. Williams has continued serving the Lord Jesus Christ as an associate pastor, a teacher, and as vice-president and representative for the Dean Burgon Society. He received a Ph.D. in Biblical studies at Louisiana Baptist University. He has traveled to many foreign lands where he has represented the Dean Burgon Society, teaching pastors and participating in evangelistic events. He is author of the several books, *The Lie That Changed The Modern World; Word-For-Word Translating of the Received Texts, Verbal Plenary Translating; Receiving, Hearing the Voice of God; The Septuagint is a Paraphrase;* and *The Attack on the Canon of Scripture* in addition to many articles and booklets. Dr. Williams and his wife, Patricia have two sons and five grandchildren.

BOOKS BY DR. WILLIAMS

HEARING THE VOICE OF GOD:
    This 264 page perfect bound book will be released in January, 2008. ISBN 978-0-9801689-0-7. You will be able to purchase it at Amazon.com. or at BibleForToday.org, BFT # **3340**.
    Dr. Williams' book, *Hearing the Voice of God,* discusses the critical factors related to the postmodern confusion surrounding this issue. He approaches the subject clearly and realistically from a biblicist's point of view. Mysticism is refuted. Individuals desiring the truth about God speaking to them will appreciate this volume. Many present day teachers cause emotionally distressed people to turn to their own thoughts, as if their thoughts were God speaking to them. This work investigates the topic as it relates to revelation, conscience, inspiration, illumination, and the voice of the Lord in Scripture. Dr. Williams explains how postmodern philosophy has created an atmosphere that contributes to the confusion surrounding this important subject. www.theoldpathspublications.com, www.biblefortoday.org.

WORD-FOR-WORD TRANSLATING OF THE RECEIVED TEXT, VERBAL PLENARY TRANSLATING:
    This 264 page perfect bound book may be purchased through www.BibleForToday.org. See below. There is a vital need for a book to inform sincere Bible-believing Christians about the proper techniques of translating the WORDS of God into the receptor languages of the world. No book like this one has ever been written. It is a unique and much-needed book. The very first requirement for any translation of the Bible is to have the proper WORDS of Hebrew, Aramaic, and Greek from which to translate. It is the contention of this book that the original verbally and plenarily inspired Hebrew, Aramaic, and Greek WORDS have been verbally and plenarily preserved in accordance with God's promises. These preserved WORDS are those received-text-WORDS which underlie the King James Bible. This volume emphasizes the requirement of a proper technique to be used in all translations of God's WORDS. It must be done in a verbally and plenarily translation technique. That is, the Hebrew, Aramaic, and Greek WORDS must be conveyed into the receptor languages, not merely the ideas, concepts, thoughts, or message. This technique is absent in all of the other manuals on Bible translation. Dr. Williams is not the usual sort of writer. He combines the meticulous skill of a Doctor of Medicine with the artistry and acumen of a Doctor of Philosophy to produce this grand volume. May translators and sincere

Christians of all persuasions and professions use this important book worldwide! The Bible For Today Press, BFT #**3302**
ISBN 1-56848-056-3, Order by PHONE: 1-800-JOHN 10:9, Order by FAX: 856-854-2464, Order by MAIL: Bible For Today, 900 Park Avenue Collingswood, NJ 08108"

THE ATTACK ON THE CANON OF SCRIPTURE, A POLEMIC AGAINST MODERN SCHOLARSHIP

This 264 page perfect bound book will be released in January, 2008. ISBN 978-0-9801689-0-7. This 152 page book demonstrates the newest attack on the Words and books of the Bible by modern day scholarship. The changing methods for assaulting the Scriptures are important for those who are concerned about the relentless attempt to destroy them. In a remarkable polemic against modern scholarship, Dr. Williams outlines the most recent means many are using to undermine confidence in the Words of God received through the priesthood of believers. It will be available at Amazon.com. or at BibleForToday.org, BFT # **3340**.

THE LIE THAT CHANGED THE MODERN WORLD

This book is in hardback format, 440 pages in all. ISBN 1-56848-042-3. It is a factual defense not only of the King James Bible, but also of the Hebrew and Greek Words that underlie the King James Bible. The author is a medical doctor, now retired, who has researched this important topic thoroughly. May the Lord Jesus Christ use and honor this study in the days, weeks, months, and years ahead until our Lord Jesus Christ returns. It should be in every layman's library, every Pastor's library, every church library, every college library, every university library, and in every theological seminary library. It is available through Bible For Today Press, www.biblefortoday.org, BFT # **3125**.

THE PURE WORDS OF GOD

This is a perfect bound 136 page book. ISBN 978-0-9801689-1-4. Dr. Williams' book, *The Pure Words of God,* clarifies the use of the word "pure" when it is used to define the Words of God. Should "pure" be applied to translations, to Traditional/Received Texts, or to critical texts? Once the correct application is explained, Dr. Williams clarifies God's commands to receive and keep His pure Words. It is available through Amazon.com or Bible For Today Press at www.biblefortoday.org, BFT #

Look for other books to be released by Dr. Williams in the near future. One work, ***The Apostolic Origin of the Traditional Text*** is nearing completion and should be released in mid-2008. Another book, ***The Septuagint is a Paraphrase***, will be release in early 2008.

www.ingramcontent.com/pod-product-compliance
Lightning Source LLC
LaVergne TN
LVHW021351080426
835508LV00020B/2221